Contents

CHAPTER 1
A WARMER WORLD

THE TINY VILLAGE OF NEWTOK, A YUP'IK COMMUNITY WITH A POPULATION OF 350, SITS ON ALASKA'S WESTERN COAST NEAR THE BERING SEA. The land here is tundra—a vast, treeless plain, dotted with ponds, splashed with lakes, and crisscrossed with rivers. Newtok rests on marshy ground between two of these rivers. The narrow Newtok River loops around the village on three sides, and the wide Ninglick River passes just south of the village on its way to the sea.

Newtok is not easy to get to. No roads link it to the outside world, not even to the closest village, which is almost 100 miles (160 kilometers) away. In winter, snowmobiles are the only way to travel between villages. In summer, travel is by boat, either on rivers or along the nearby coast. Yup'ik people have been living in the area for two thousand years, carrying out a way of life tied to the seasons and the cycles of fishing, hunting, and foraging. They have maintained their traditions across generations, aided by their isolation. Over the last two decades, though, the town has grown unsafe.

Newtok is perched atop permafrost, ground that has remained frozen for at least two years. Permafrost underlies much of the Arctic, as well as about 80 percent of the state of Alaska. In these areas, 1 to 2 feet (0.3–0.6 meters) of surface soil may freeze and thaw throughout the year, but beneath that top layer, permafrost hundreds or thousands of feet thick stays frozen. Or at least it used to. Because of climate change, temperatures in Alaska are rising, and widespread areas of permafrost are thawing. As a result, the ground under Newtok has turned soft and mushy. The entire village is crooked. Homes slump, telephone poles tilt at odd angles, and boardwalks are sinking into the mire. Meanwhile, climate change is dramatically speeding up the rate of erosion, causing the wide Ninglick River to

Residents of Newtok, Alaska, rely on wooden boardwalks to get around the eroding, flood-plagued village. Extreme weather and rising tides have made the village increasingly unsafe.

shift closer to the village. Between 1954 and 2001, the river washed away more than 4,000 feet (1,219 m) of riverbank. That's the length of eleven football fields laid end to end.

Vast slabs of sea ice used to protect the coastline from strong autumn storms. But in recent decades, that ice has formed increasingly later in the year. Because of the shorter ice season, storm waves surge up the Ninglick River, claw at the softening riverbank, and carry away chunks of land. Between 1957 and 2003, the Ninglick River swallowed an average of 71 feet (22 m) of bank—nearly the length of a high school basketball court—per year. Some years it carried away much more. A combination of erosion and extreme weather has damaged the village landfill, the sewage treatment area, and the fuel storage facility. The Ninglick's advance also encroached on the narrow Newtok River, where residents had long emptied human waste. By 1996 the Newtok River had transformed into a swampy backwater, making the village more prone to floods and causing raw sewage to linger dangerously close to the village. In 2005 the Ninglick demolished the landing area for the barge that delivers essential supplies and fuel in summer. In August 2006, a barge bringing much-needed fuel became stranded for three days. Emergency fuel had to be flown into the village.

During a storm the year before, rising waters completely surrounded Newtok, turning the village into an island for several days. The flooding submerged boardwalks, destroyed food storage facilities, shut down utilities, spread sewage-laced floodwater throughout the community, and displaced people from their homes. In a 2009 report, the US Army Corps of Engineers declared that Newtok was no longer safe. Within ten or fifteen years, the report concluded, the village would be destroyed. There was no way to protect the village in its current location. Staying in Newtok was not an option.

Scientists say Newtok citizens' experience will soon become a global phenomenon. As climate change drastically alters the planet,

Disaster-Induced Displacement Worldwide in One Year

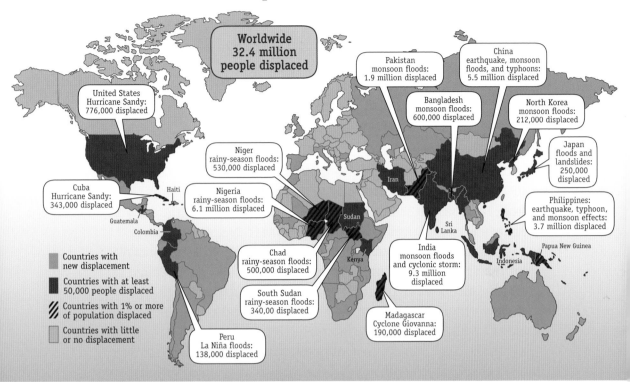

Worldwide
32.4 million
people displaced

United States
Hurricane Sandy:
776,000 displaced

Cuba
Hurricane Sandy:
343,000 displaced

Haiti

Guatemala

Colombia

Pakistan
monsoon floods:
1.9 million displaced

China
earthquake, monsoon
floods, and typhoons:
5.5 million displaced

Bangladesh
monsoon floods:
600,000 displaced

North Korea
monsoon floods:
212,000 displaced

Japan
floods and
landslides:
250,000
displaced

Philippines:
earthquake, typhoon,
and monsoon effects:
3.7 million displaced

Iran

Niger
rainy-season floods:
530,000 displaced

Nigeria
rainy-season floods:
6.1 million displaced

Sudan

Sri
Lanka

Papua New Guinea

Chad
rainy-season floods:
500,000 displaced

Kenya

India
monsoon floods
and cyclonic storm:
9.3 million
displaced

Indonesia

South Sudan
rainy-season floods:
340,00 displaced

Madagascar
Cyclone Giovanna:
190,000 displaced

Peru
La Niña floods:
138,000 displaced

Countries with
new displacement

Countries with at least
50,000 people displaced

Countries with 1% or more
of population displaced

Countries with little
or no displacement

Each year, natural disasters displace millions of people—some temporarily, some permanently. As climate change accelerates, the frequency and intensity of natural disasters increase in many areas. This map shows where and why people were displaced by natural disasters in the year 2012.

more places will become unlivable and millions of people all over the world will become climate migrants—people who are forced to flee their homes due to the effects of a changing environment.

Climate Change and the Greenhouse Effect

Climate change is nothing new. Over the past two million years, huge ice sheets—massive layers of ice—have spread over Earth and retreated numerous times. Scientists generally agree that these cycles—cold glacial periods alternating with warm interglacial periods—are triggered by regular, small changes in Earth's orbit. Experts study the planet's climate history through evidence in fossils, tree rings, deep-sea sediments, and ice cores (segments of glacial ice).

Climate change in the twentieth and twenty-first centuries, scientists say, is different. This time, the climate is changing mainly because of human activities, particularly the burning of fossil fuels—energy sources formed from the remains of ancient plants. Coal, oil or petroleum, and natural gas are fossil fuels. When burned, they release carbon dioxide into the air. From the beginnings of the industrial revolution in the late 1700s, machines powered by fossil fuels have driven the advance of human industry. Yet the burning of fossil fuels has put billions of tons of carbon dioxide into the air. This has created a significant and serious change in Earth's atmosphere.

The atmosphere is a mixture of invisible gases: large amounts of nitrogen and oxygen mixed with much smaller amounts of carbon dioxide, methane, ozone, and water vapor. Each day, sunlight passes through this invisible mixture and warms the land and water. Some of the heat is reflected back into space.

In the late 1850s, an Irish physicist named John Tyndall discovered that nitrogen and oxygen allow light and heat to pass through these gases freely. But other gases—such as carbon dioxide and water vapor—block the escaping heat. Tyndall realized what this meant. Although the heat-blocking gases were present in the air only in tiny amounts, they were largely responsible for setting the planet's thermostat.

The heat-trapping phenomenon that Tyndall studied came to be known as the natural greenhouse effect. The effect is similar to the warming that occurs inside a locked car in the sun. The glass of the car windows allows sunlight to enter but prevents heat from escaping. Heat builds up inside. The natural greenhouse effect creates the conditions for life on Earth as we know it. Without it, the planet's average surface temperature would be only about 0°F (−18°C), instead of approximately 60°F (15°C).

In the 1890s, Swedish scientist Svante Arrhenius followed up on Tyndall's work by calculating how the planet's temperature would be affected by different levels of carbon dioxide. From those calculations, Arrhenius realized that people could enhance the natural greenhouse effect by adding carbon dioxide to the air. By the late nineteenth century, factories and trains all over the industrialized world were burning coal and belching out smoke laced with carbon dioxide. Arrhenius predicted that this widespread burning of coal and the release of carbon dioxide could, over a long period of time, warm the planet.

Throughout the twentieth century, industrialized nations burned more and more fossil fuels, and carbon dioxide steadily accumulated in the air. In the 1950s, an American chemist named Charles Keeling decided to measure the amount of carbon dioxide in the atmosphere. At a weather observatory on Mauna Loa, a volcano on the island

What's Up with the Weather?

People often confuse weather and climate. The difference between the two is time. Weather is the day-to-day conditions in a particular area. For example, one day could be sunny, and the next could be overcast with a downpour. Climate is the long-term pattern of weather, often measured over a period of thirty years. For example, you can expect snow to fall in New England during winter. The southwestern United States is likely to sizzle in the summer. These are recurring patterns.

If a blizzard slams the city of Boston, Massachusetts, some people may argue that this is evidence that the planet isn't warming. But a single storm is a weather event, not a reflection of the overall climate. Therefore, it doesn't disprove climate change, just as a sizzling day in Phoenix, Arizona, doesn't prove climate change.

Climate change is slow. Each decade becomes a little warmer than the one before it. And while the planet is heating up overall, climate change can trigger extreme weather patterns of all sorts, including cold fronts and blizzards. If the number of severe hot days in Phoenix—or the number of severe storms in Boston—gradually climbs over a number of years, that can be an indication of climate change.

of Hawaii, he began to take daily measurements of carbon dioxide. These measurements, which became known as the Keeling Curve, show that carbon dioxide levels fall in the summer, when plants in the Northern Hemisphere absorb carbon dioxide for photosynthesis (the process by which plants create food). Levels rise in the winter, when these plants are not carrying out photosynthesis. Because of this annual rise and fall, the Keeling Curve looks like the edge of a saw, with a jagged tooth corresponding to each year.

The Keeling Curve revealed something else. It showed for the first time that carbon dioxide in the atmosphere was steadily rising. In 1959, the first year of the Mauna Loa recordings, the annual mean (the average of the summer and winter measurements) was 316 parts per million (a measurement for very diluted substances) of carbon dioxide in the atmosphere. The next year, carbon dioxide was 317 parts per million. It was up to 325 parts per million by 1970, 354 parts per million by 1990, and 400 parts per million by 2013. Climatologists say this is the highest level of carbon dioxide the world has seen in three million years. In 2014 people pumped more than 39 billion tons (35.7 billion metric tons) of carbon dioxide into the air by burning coal, oil, and natural gas.

Numerous modern scientific studies have confirmed what Arrhenius predicted: the buildup of carbon dioxide is heating the planet. Earth's atmosphere has warmed by 1.4°F (0.8°C) since the 1880s. This may not seem like much, but it is enough to melt glaciers and ice caps, raise sea levels, and change weather patterns worldwide, forcing human communities to migrate.

The Melting Arctic

The snow and ice at the North Pole are frozen ocean, not land. Every year this blanket of sea ice grows and shrinks. Each winter the ice grows. In summer, as temperatures rise above freezing, it melts. Some of that ice, called perennial sea ice, survives the summer and remains year-round. Since the late 1970s, warmer temperatures have caused the Arctic's perennial sea ice to shrink dramatically. Satellite images show the ice's decline. In 2012 the sea ice shrank to the smallest size ever recorded, just half the size it had been thirty years earlier. At the same time, the winter ice has thinned and weakened.

Most of the world's glaciers—large masses of ice on land, many of them thousands of years old—are also shrinking. Evidence for this is especially stark on the continent of Antarctica and on the large Arctic island of Greenland. Both land masses are almost completely covered by ice sheets—enormous layers of glacier ice. The Greenland ice sheet is nearly the same land area as the entire state of Alaska. The Antarctic ice sheet is about the same land area as the continental United States and Mexico combined. Both ice sheets show unmistakable signs of melting: shrinking in area and dwindling in mass, with huge chunks of ice breaking off at the edges.

Although climate change is happening across the globe, the Arctic is heating up twice as fast as the rest of the world. According to Douglas Causey, a professor of biology at the University of Alaska–Anchorage, "The Arctic is the place that's reacting the fastest and in the largest way [to climate change]." In addition to the thawing of

The Ripple of Arctic Changes

Changes in the Arctic can disrupt weather thousands of miles away—partly because of the Arctic's effect on the jet stream. This current of air flows eastward in a wavy pattern around the globe, affecting weather patterns in the Northern Hemisphere. Some climatologists think that as the Arctic warms, the changing temperature is making the jet stream weaker and wavier, with higher peaks and lower valleys. This may be causing weather patterns such as droughts, heat waves, and cold spells to last longer, especially in North America and Europe.

permafrost, snow cover is declining, tundra is drying out, wildfires are breaking out in increasingly dry areas every summer, and ponds and streams are drying up and disappearing. As the sea ice recedes, seals, walruses, and other animals that depend on it are retreating too. As temperatures warm, moose are moving north. Caribou and salmon are disappearing from their normal ranges and seeking new territories. Across the tundra, certain species of berries and other plants are disappearing, replaced by shrubs and trees.

These changes put a profound strain on the indigenous peoples of the Arctic, many of whom move between seasonal camps and rely on hunting, fishing, and foraging for food. "The sea ice used to take longer to melt. It lasted about ten months," said Charlie Nakqashuk from the Canadian territory of Nunavut, "but now it's only eight months. This harms our way of life, our way of hunting, our way of fishing, and our way of traveling from one place to another." Melting ice and snow cause shifts in animals' ranges, often driving them farther from people and making hunting more difficult.

Vanishing Villages

The ripples of climate change are creating waves of Arctic climate migrants. Indigenous peoples are particularly vulnerable. Of 213 Native Alaskan villages, 86 percent face flooding and erosion, mainly caused by melting sea ice and thawing permafrost. Four Native Alaskan villages—Newtok, Kivalina, Koyukuk, and Shishmaref—are at immediate risk of disappearing altogether.

As of 2015, Koyukuk leaders are in the early stages of planning the community's relocation. Shishmaref and Kivalina leaders are working with state and federal officials on plans to move. However, they have had trouble obtaining enough funding and finding a suitable new location. Both communities have proposed new sites, but the federal government has deemed those locations unsafe. Melting permafrost makes the land unstable and unsuitable for supporting buildings.

Feedback Loops

Positive feedback loops—when a small change cascades through a system and leads to even bigger changes—are accelerating climate change. For example, as Earth's air warms, it can hold more moisture, leading to heavier precipitation (rain and snow). Water vapor is itself a potent greenhouse gas, so moisture in the air warms the planet further. Another feedback loop involves ancient carbon that is locked in Arctic ice and permafrost. As the Arctic warms and the ice and permafrost melt, these ancient stores of carbon escape into the air as either carbon dioxide or methane. These greenhouse gases contribute to more warming, which in turn drives more melting and further release of trapped gases as the cycle continues.

Yet another positive feedback loop involves albedo. Albedo is the amount of sunlight that reflects off a surface instead of being absorbed. Each surface has a different albedo, a measure of whiteness (*alb* means "white"). For example, dark surfaces have a low albedo. Their reflectivity is low, and they absorb plenty of energy from the sun. By contrast, lighter-colored surfaces have a higher albedo and mostly reflect sunlight. These surfaces therefore stay cooler.

Albedo has significant consequences as the Arctic thaws. Bright, white ice and snow have a high albedo. As sea ice melts, the bright, shiny surface turns into dark water. As snow and ice on land melt, the snow-white surface becomes darker tundra. In both cases, the albedo of Earth's surface decreases. Dark open water and tundra absorb more heat from the sun. As a result, the surface and air temperatures of the region rise. These rising temperatures cause more ice and snow to melt, allowing more sunlight to be absorbed, leading to even more warming.

The only community that has made progress so far is Newtok. In 1996 the residents voted to abandon their village and move to a new site located 9 miles (14 km) away across the Ninglick River. (They voted in favor of the move again in 2001 and 2003.) The new site, called Mertarvik, is perched on a rise above the river, safe above the waves. It sits on solid bedrock, not permafrost.

Despite this step forward, the move has hit many roadblocks. Before people could begin moving, the community had to oversee the building of homes, roads, and other infrastructure at the new location. About one-third of the sixty-three homes in Newtok can be moved. The rest are being replaced with new structures at the Mertarvik site. No unified government program exists to organize and fund the relocation of a community. Villagers must put together funding from various state and federal agencies. Relocation is not cheap. The US Army Corps of Engineers estimated the costs of relocating Newtok at $80 million to $130 million. That works out to about $228,000 to $371,000 per person.

The village of Kivalina is connected to the Alaskan mainland by a narrow strip of shoreline, which is shrinking due to erosion. Kivalina's four hundred residents hope to relocate before the entire settlement is washed away.

Turning misfortune into opportunity, seventeen villagers spent four months learning construction skills at a school in a distant town so they would be able to help with the rebuilding process. Still, long winters and short summers make for a short construction season. Progress remains slow, with only three homes built by mid-2015. The main priority is a partially finished evacuation center, powered by a community solar array and wind farm. Newtok residents can seek shelter at the center if the old village floods before relocation is complete.

The community is in a race against time. Experts predict that the old village will be washed away by 2019, if not sooner. "Most people can't wait till we move across [to the new village]," said Lisa Charles, who will move to the new site with her husband, Jeff, and their six children. "I know that it will eventually happen, but we're just not sure when or how long we'll have to wait. I hope that things will speed up before it's too late, before the erosion gets too close to the houses."

In Search of Shelter

You don't need to live in the Arctic to experience climate change or the reality of climate migration. In small island countries, on coasts, and along rivers around the world, humans are already fleeing rising seas, severe storms, and desertification (drying out of land). In many parts of Asia, Africa, North America, and South America, melting glaciers and deepening drought (temporary periods with little rainfall) threaten food and water supplies. For instance, South Asian countries face devastating droughts that alternate with massive floods. Large areas of North and Central America are plagued by extremely dry conditions, with some experts predicting future megadroughts that could last at least thirty years.

In the continental United States, climate change's effects include unusually high levels of precipitation, extreme summertime heat, devastating floods, and severe droughts. The average temperature in the United States has risen by 1.3°F to 1.9°F (0.7°C to 1.1°C) since 1895, with most of this increase occurring since about 1970.

Yup'ik Traditions and Climate Change

Ina Bouker, an elementary and high school teacher, and her daughter, Nia White, a student at the University of Alaska–Anchorage, both grew up in the Bristol Bay area of Alaska. They follow the traditional Yup'ik way of life by hunting, fishing, and foraging. Those traditions are being affected by climate change. Bouker recalls,

> When I was young, our family would move seasonally depending on where the animals were. In the springtime, we'd go to where all the herring fish and the herring eggs were being spawned [laid]. Then we'd move over to where all our salmon would be coming through, up the river. Later on in the summer, we moved further up to where all the berries are so we could do our berry harvest. Then in the fall, we go up to the lake where the salmon already had spawned, and we would catch those and dry them. Then we'd go back to the main village right before school starts. From there we would do our moose hunting [we'd hunt] caribou, beaver, rabbits, ptarmigan [a type of bird] as winter comes [and] geese as they're flying south.

Bouker teaches grades kindergarten through twelve at the local school. In addition to passing on Yup'ik traditions such as dancing, drumming, singing, and storytelling, she teaches her students how to wisely use the land's natural resources. "I bring in animals and cut those up in front of them and teach them how to process the animals and the berries. I bring them out berry picking. We make jelly. We make jam. We often have tasting parties with dried fish, seal oil, seal meat, dried meat, and herring eggs."

Recently, however, Bouker and White have both noticed the effects of climate change on these once reliable food sources. White notes, "There's basically no snow in the winter now. The loss of snow pack is affecting the tundra, drying it out." This makes it harder for certain plants to grow. "We're not getting the same amount of berries that we usually do."

Fishing is an important part of the traditional Yup'ik way of life. In recent years, however, climate change has altered the migration patterns of fish, making fishing more difficult for Native Alaskans.

Consequences for animal life are equally stark. Bouker says,

> Our moose population is moving to different areas, and areas that didn't used to have a lot of moose now have a lot of moose. The fish travel patterns are changing depending on the water temperature and the sand. Out in our bay, there are big sand bars. With the water rising, those sand bars are changing, so some of the fish are being channeled to other rivers that they don't normally go to. . . . The birds—the geese, the duck, the cranes, the swans—are also moving to different areas because of the water level. The tundra is so dry, but at the same time the rivers are overflowing. Our bay is rising, and the storms are coming up to our cabins, so we are having to move some of the cabins further up the beach.

Wildfires are becoming increasingly common in parts of the western United States as climate change contributes to drier conditions. In September 2015, a wildfire in Northern California destroyed more than one thousand homes. Experts believe record numbers of people may be displaced by climate-related disasters in the coming decades.

This may seem like only a small upward shift, but Americans in the mountainous West are facing water shortages and more frequent wildfires as a result of the change. The Southwest too is experiencing increasingly severe drought and wildfires. The Northeast and Southeast are seeing extreme heat, with heavier downpours in the Northeast and water shortages in the Southeast. Extreme storms and flooding will batter low-lying coastal areas around the country. This means that some areas of the United States are becoming dangerous places to live—and these conditions may eventually drive out many residents. Other areas, away from coasts and deserts, will draw climate migrants from around the country, as well as migrants arriving from outside the United States.

Humanity's response to climate change can follow two paths: mitigation and adaptation. Mitigation involves reducing the extent and speed of climate change by targeting the root of the problem:

greenhouse gas emissions. Actions such as using alternative energy sources fit into this category.

Adaptation involves reducing vulnerability to the changes that are already occurring. This might mean building walls to protect a coastal village from rising seas. Or it could mean planting trees on dry farmland to anchor the soil and improve crop yields. It might even require relocating an entire community to a safer spot. The best adaptation strategies are flexible, allowing communities to evolve as climate change proceeds, believes Robin Bronen, head of the Alaska Immigration Justice Project. In many areas, even the most advanced measures will provide only temporary solutions. "At one point in time, it might be determined that protecting the community in place is a good strategy," said Bronen in 2015. "But let's say two years from now, a severe storm comes in, and it's no longer viable to protect this community in place based on the damage. So we [would] need to shift to managed retreat or long-term relocation." Migration is a form of adaptation in its own right—usually a last resort for people whose communities have reached a crisis point.

With climate change progressing at great speed, large numbers of climate migrants are moving within their home countries. Often they are relocating from rural areas to cities in search of a sustainable future. Migration across international borders is also increasing. In the coming decades, wealthy developed nations, such as Australia, the United States, and many European countries, are especially likely to face an influx of migrants from other continents, such as Africa and Asia. Based on current climate scenarios, experts believe the twenty-first century will see migration on a massive scale, with more people on the move than at any other time in human history. Climate migration will touch the lives of everyone on the planet.

CHAPTER 2
RISING TIDES

THE THIRTY-THREE TINY ISLANDS OF THE REPUBLIC OF KIRIBATI ARE SCATTERED ACROSS THE MIDDLE OF THE PACIFIC OCEAN. They spread across 1.3 million square miles (3.4 million sq. km) of ocean, an area nearly twice the size of Alaska. From the air, the republic's islands look as though they barely rise above the turquoise sea. In fact, most of South Tarawa, the capital, is less than 10 feet (3 m) above sea level. All but one of Kiribati's islands sit at less than 30 feet (9 m) above sea level. Fifty thousand people—nearly half of Kiribati's population—live on less than 6 square miles (15 sq. km) of land. Scientists, political leaders, and the republic's citizens, known as the I-Kiribati, are concerned about the effect of climate change on their low-lying islands. Sea levels are already rising, and scientists project that sea levels could rise by another 3 feet (1 m) by the end of the century—possibly sooner—making much of Kiribati unlivable.

Many island nations around the world are similarly vulnerable to the impact of climate change. At particularly high risk are coral atolls—flat, ring-shaped islands made of sand and other debris perched on top of coral reefs (rock formed from the skeletons of small sea creatures called coral). Along with Kiribati, these atoll nations include Pacific Ocean countries such as the Marshall Islands and Tuvalu, as well as the Maldives in the Indian Ocean. On these small, flat island chains, residents have nowhere to retreat as the seas rise.

Ice Sheets and Rising Seas

The planet's sea level has remained almost steady for thousands of years, until the average surface level of the world's oceans began to rise in the late nineteenth century. During the twentieth century, the world's oceans rose by about 8 inches (20 centimeters) due to climate change. Climate change causes seas to rise in two ways: by

The village of Eita in the Pacific island nation of Kiribati was largely submerged by flooding in September 2015. Rising sea levels endanger the survival of Kiribati, which may be almost completely underwater within a few decades.

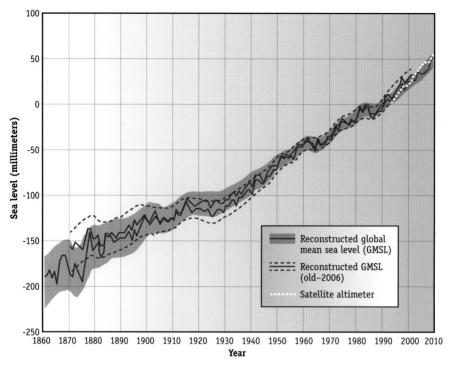

Since the mid-1800s, the global average sea level (also called global mean sea level, or GMSL) has risen at an increasing rate. Sea level can be measured in many different ways. The dark gray and red solid lines represent data from devices called tide gauges. The white dotted line beginning in the 1990s represents satellite data. The red dashed lines and the light gray band show the margins for error.

warming the ocean and by melting ice on land. As Earth's surface temperature rises, the oceans absorb a lot of this additional heat. Water increases in volume as it warms. This is called thermal expansion, and it accounts for about half of the current rise in sea level. In addition, water from melting mountain glaciers and ice sheets runs off into the ocean, further raising the level of the sea.

While some rise in sea level is inevitable, experts remain uncertain how much—and, equally significant, how fast—the oceans will rise due to climate change. The answer depends on what will happen to the ice in Greenland and Antarctica. Each of these land masses is buried under a permanent ice sheet. The vast layer of thick ice is formed from old snow that under the weight of fresh layers of snow has been pressed to ice. How much and how fast the seas rise depends on how much these ice sheets melt. Richard Alley, a glaciologist at Pennsylvania State University who studies climate change, says this hinges on the stability of ice shelves. An ice shelf is the part of an ice sheet that extends over the ocean, usually in a bay or a fjord (a long, narrow inlet of sea between high cliffs). Normally, friction between the ice shelf and the rocky shoreline holds the shelf in place. But as the ice shelf melts, it shrinks and pulls back from the shoreline. Without the friction, melting ice flows more rapidly into the sea, where it can break off and raise sea levels.

Predicting what will happen to ice shelves is challenging, partly because it depends on ocean currents, which are in turn affected by climate change. "The melting part is easy," says Alley. "It gets warmer [which leads to] more melt. How does the ocean bring heat under these floating ice shelves? And how does the ocean circulation work? [That] is actually very hard [to predict]."

The United Nation's (UN) Intergovernmental Panel on Climate Change (IPCC), an international scientific body that reports on climate change and its impacts, projects that Earth's seas will likely rise an additional 9 to 11 inches (24 to 29 cm) by 2050 and 17 to 29 inches (44 to 74 cm) by 2100. If the ice shelves melt, seas could rise much higher—and much faster: up to 6 feet (1.8 m) by the century's end.

Uninhabitable Islands

The increase in sea level is making life difficult on island nations such as Kiribati. Rising oceans cause flooding when they combine with extreme high-water events. These include high waves from a storm or seasonal high tides, known as king tides, which usually wash ashore about twice a year. Because of rising seas, king tides and other high-water events are higher than in the past. Floodwater breaches seawalls, submerges roads, and swamps houses.

The rising ocean is poisoning freshwater supplies on low-lying islands around the world. Freshwater is scarce in Kiribati. Islanders collect water from a freshwater lens, a layer of rainwater that forms about 6 feet (2 m) under the ground and floats on top of the salt water there. But water from the rising ocean is percolating into the lens. This phenomenon is called saltwater intrusion, and it makes the limited water supplies too salty to drink.

Increasing amounts of salt water are poisoning the soil, killing trees, and making it harder for the I-Kiribati to grow food. "When the tide is up [the water] really runs through the sand and kills everything," says Jack Joe, who lives on the island of North Tarawa and describes the difficulties of growing backyard vegetables. "Cabbages and tomatoes, things like that. Cucumbers. Gone." A few dead vegetable plants may not seem like a big deal, but the people of Kiribati rely on vegetables from their family gardens to supplement their fish-based diet. Land suitable for growing crops is already in short supply in Kiribati because of poor soil and the islands' small size. Loss of local cropland forces islanders to import food from elsewhere, and many Kiribati households spend more than half of their budgets on groceries.

Climate change also jeopardizes the local food supply indirectly by harming the nearby coral reefs, which provide a habitat for fish. Ocean warming and ocean acidification damage reefs by making corals more brittle and more prone to diseases and slowing the rate at which they can build and repair themselves. In addition to endangering fish habitats and threatening an important food source for islanders, reef damage compromises an important layer of protection against erosion and flooding on land.

As the seas continue to rise, grow warmer, and become more acidic, residents of island nations will be the first people to bear the full brunt of those changes. The resulting damage could eventually make these places unlivable.

Growing or Shrinking?

Inhabitants of Pacific island nations such as Kiribati fear that their island homes could disappear completely, submerged under

Climate Change's "Evil Twin"

Since the beginning of the industrial revolution, the oceans have naturally absorbed about 525 billion tons (476 metric tons) of carbon dioxide—almost half of the carbon dioxide produced by fossil fuels—from the atmosphere. This process is known as ocean acidification. Marine biologist Jane Lubchenco, a former head of the National Oceanic and Atmospheric Administration, calls ocean acidification "climate change's equally evil twin." When carbon dioxide dissolves in water, it changes the ocean's chemistry. The water becomes more acidic, and the ocean's pH drops. (Scientists use the pH scale to measure how basic or acidic ocean water is.) Ocean acidification has serious consequences for marine life. A drop in pH can inhibit shell growth in animals such as corals, oysters, shrimp, and lobsters. For three hundred million years, ocean pH has averaged about 8.2. Since the early 1800s, it has dropped from an average of 8.2 to around 8.1. This drop of 0.1 pH units represents a 25 percent increase in acidity, which is enough to dissolve the shells of some sea animals. According to projections, ocean pH could drop by another 0.5 pH units by the end of the twenty-first century, a change that would upset ocean food webs and harm fish populations, threatening a food source for millions of people. When people lose a crucial local food source such as fish, they are often forced to relocate.

rapidly rising ocean waters. In Kiribati an entire village and several additional homes have already been lost to the sea, forcing residents to move inland. Two uninhabited islets—Tebua Tarawa and Abanuea—vanished under the waves in the 1990s. Yet scientists disagree over whether rising seas are to blame for these particular losses. While it's clear that the ocean is rising, human activities also affect Kiribati's shorelines. "Pictures of flooding you see on the news have more to do with poor shoreline management and people settling on marginal land than with sea-level rise," says Simon Donner, a climate scientist at the University of British Columbia in Canada who researches the effects of climate change on Kiribati.

Although scientists generally agree that rising seas pose a grave threat to island nations—through flooding, saltwater intrusion, and damage to coral reefs—not all scientists think the islands will be lost under the waves. Some point out that coral atolls may actually grow. When high water swirls over atolls, it washes sand formed from broken coral, shell fragments, and other debris onto the land. That sand raises the islands' elevation— often at a rate that outpaces the speed of sea level rise. "As long as the [coral] reef is healthy and generates an abundant supply of sand, there's no reason a reef island can't grow and keep up," says evolution and landform expert Paul Kench of the University of Auckland in New Zealand. Other scientists dismiss the idea that Kiribati and other islands will grow enough to keep pace with the rising water. Coral atolls do grow, they say, but oceans are expected to rise so rapidly over the upcoming century that the islands can't possibly keep up. Furthermore, many experts argue that with the health of coral reefs in jeopardy due to ocean acidification, atoll growth rates are far from guaranteed.

To study whether atolls have shrunk as the seas have risen, researchers compared recent aerial photographs of Pacific islands with photographs of the same islands taken decades earlier. They studied twenty-seven islands across Kiribati, Tuvalu, and the Federated States of Micronesia. Of those islands, twenty-three had either grown in area or remained the same, while only four had shrunk.

In any case, the islands are changing as the oceans change, and where people can live safely on the islands is changing too. "It's a slow onset," explains Maldives activist Thilmeeza Hussain. "For example, people living closest to the beach, their houses may get washed away by a storm, but nobody's talking about it because it's just one or two houses. But what do they do? It's a small country and we don't have homeowner's insurance. People spend their whole life savings to build these homes and they're left with nothing [after a storm]."

Anote Tong, who served as president of the Republic of Kiribati from 2003 to 2016, made climate change the focus of his administration. In 2014 he visited a shrinking Arctic glacier in Norway to explore the link between melting glaciers and rising sea level, which endangers his small nation of Pacific islands.

"The Human Face of Climate Change"

Leaders of Pacific island nations, seeking support from other countries, find themselves performing a difficult dance on the world stage. On the one hand, they emphasize that they are unwilling to move and that they have a right to stay. Moving to a different country would mean losing a vital link to their identity and their culture. It would also be a blow to their sovereignty—their status as a self-governing nation. Yet even as they assert the importance of remaining in their homelands, these leaders are being forced to consider the possibility of relocation for the safety of their people. That means asserting their people's right to be accommodated by another country if the rising seas force evacuation.

No one knows whether the I-Kiribati will be able to remain on their islands or whether they will have to leave. But the republic's former president Anote Tong thinks that the islands will be uninhabitable by around 2030. "We will lose our homeland unless the ocean stops rising," he stated bluntly in a 2014 interview while still in office. The people of Kiribati understand what is coming, says Tong, but they don't want to leave. "It's very simple. We want to stay home. This is where the spirits live. This is where we're from."

Tong travels the world, speaking about the plight of his country and advocating for action on climate change. "The people of my country are already feeling the impacts of climate change, which will only worsen with time," Tong told the UN General Assembly in 2009. "We, together with [the citizens] of other low-lying states, are the human face of climate change."

Building Resilience

For the most part, the environmental degradation in the Pacific will be gradual, giving island nations time to plan ahead. Pacific Islanders have a long history of adapting to changing conditions. With a combination of local knowledge and outside resources, countries can create programs and infrastructure that will help offset the effects of climate change. These kinds of measures can build climate resilience—the ability to function successfully despite the challenges of an altered environment. Adaptation may stave off the need for evacuation. For Pacific Islanders, possible resilience measures include improving rainwater harvesting, building seawalls, planting trees to guard against erosion, and evacuating particularly flood-prone areas. The Kiribati Adaptation Program, funded by several international organizations, is working to implement many of these projects. However, efforts to act quickly and minimize expenses can easily create complications. In 2011 the program built several seawalls on the islands. Project leaders chose a simple, inexpensive seawall design, instead of a more expensive design that would have made the walls stronger and more durable. Just a few months after the project's completion, waves and erosion had already damaged the new seawalls. Workers had to repair and improve the seawalls using a modified design. Project leaders hope to learn from this experience, which illustrates the need for sufficient funding, thorough planning, and long-term commitment for adaptation measures to succeed.

Leaving Home

If evacuation of Pacific islands becomes necessary, world leaders must consider where Pacific island migrants will go. Cities in nearby nations, such as Australia and New Zealand, will likely draw large numbers of people. However, resettlement is expensive. A UN study released in 2015 found that only one-quarter of the households in the island nations of Kiribati, Nauru, and Tuvalu could actually afford a move without financial assistance. In cases of cross-border relocation, governments must decide who pays for migrants' transportation and new accommodations, as well as health care, education, and job training once the migrants arrive in their new homes. Should Pacific island nations bear these costs for their people? Some observers say no. After all, Pacific island countries produce just a

Global Carbon Dioxide Emissions from Fossil Fuels

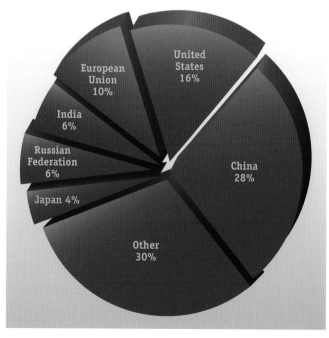

A few nations produce a vast majority of the world's carbon dioxide emissions. In 2011, the year this chart's data was collected, China's emissions rivaled the combined emissions of more than 160 other nations (in the "Other" category). Other top emitters included the United States and the countries of the European Union (EU).

sliver—0.04 percent—of the world's total greenhouse gas emissions. "The people in the South Pacific hardly contribute anything to global climate change," writes Volker Boege, an expert on conflict and peace building at the University of Queensland in Australia. "But they are left with all the problems, including losing their entire homelands. That is just not fair." Many experts argue that the burden of paying should fall on the countries that contribute the most to climate change by releasing high levels of greenhouse gas emissions. However, these wealthy nations are reluctant to redirect funds that currently go toward other security priorities. "With limited resources, we must ask if [climate change aid] best meets our national security interests," said Ileana Ros-Lehtinen, chairwoman of the US House of Representatives Foreign Affairs Committee.

Meanwhile, climate migrants who can afford to relocate often struggle to navigate other nations' immigration policies. They face questions about their status once they arrive. International refugee law does not recognize climate migrants as refugees, a category that would grant them specific protections under the law, such as protection from forcible return to the area from which they fled. According to the United Nations 1951 Refugee Convention, the term *refugee* applies strictly to a person forced to cross an international border while fleeing persecution because of his or her race, religion, nationality, or political stance. People fleeing sea level rise, disappearing islands, erosion, and other effects of climate change do not fit that legal definition.

In 2014 a family from the island nation of Tuvalu was granted asylum (legal protection that a nation grants to a refugee) in New Zealand. It was the first successful case of asylum being granted to someone fleeing the effects of climate change. The couple had moved to New Zealand in 2007. Their two children were born there, but the family had no legal status in New Zealand as of 2009. The family pursued legal refugee status, arguing that they would face danger from climate change if forced to return to Tuvalu. When the New Zealand immigration court ruled in the family's favor, it took into account other humanitarian issues. For instance, the family had relatives living in New Zealand, including an elderly mother who required care.

Although the New Zealand ruling was groundbreaking, it does not make New Zealand a welcoming destination for all climate change migrants. In the same year the Tuvalu family was granted asylum, New Zealand's high court rejected a Kiribati man's bid for asylum for him and his family. He too argued that his family would face serious harm if forced to return to Kiribati.

Media coverage dubbed Kiribati citizen Ioane Teitiota the first climate migrant for his failed attempt to secure asylum in New Zealand. He and his wife and children were deported from New Zealand and reluctantly returned to Kiribati in 2015.

The UN classification system does not recognize climate migrants as refugees. "We have to be realistic about what countries want," said Dina Ionesco of the International Organization for Migration (IOM) in 2013. "At the moment they're not interested in changing [the official terminology], so we are not trying to push that." Still, as increasingly dire climate-related situations force more and more people to move, many activists and experts are calling for world leaders to reevaluate the needs and rights of climate migrants. Rather than simply pressing for a change in the legal status of climate migrants, the IOM and other advocacy groups are encouraging governments to expand existing aid programs and policies to include climate migrants. Ionesco added, "You can and must look at the issue from the perspective of human rights and protect the rights of migrants in every situation."

"Migration with Dignity"

The prospect of resettling entire countries raises other thorny questions. Will island countries remain independent nations, or will they simply cease to exist? Will the relocated people retain their original citizenship, become citizens of the new country, or have no citizenship at all? Will their people be able to preserve their traditional lifestyle and their culture?

During his time as president of Kiribati, Anote Tong pursued a policy of "migration with dignity" for the 103,000 citizens of his country. He wants migrating islanders to be able to get jobs, move gradually, adapt to a new culture, and help build a new Kiribati community elsewhere. So he is encouraging his citizens to learn useful skills that will prepare them for life outside the republic.

Young people are leading the way. One experimental program, the Kiribati Australia Nursing Initiative (KANI), gives scholarships to young I-Kiribati to study nursing in the large metropolitan area of Brisbane, Australia. The program helps address a severe nursing shortage in Australia by training people from Kiribati to fill those jobs. It also provides a preview of what the realities of long-term relocation may hold for the I-Kiribati.

Culture clashes and homesickness are common experiences for the nursing students. Most I-Kiribati grow up in an extended family living together under one roof. Everybody sleeps on woven mats on the floor. They eat meals sitting on the floor. But students in the KANI program must adapt to an urban, Western lifestyle. They live with host families in the suburbs, where they are expected to sleep in beds and eat at tables. Many students say they miss their families and their islands. But the promise of a job and the possibility of

Pacific island nations imperiled by rising seas have frequently called for wealthier nations to help address the issue of climate change. In 2009 government officials from the Republic of the Maldives held an underwater meeting to call attention to the plight of their island country. Ibrahim Didi (IN YELLOW MASK), the minister of fisheries and agriculture, urged the UN to take action to curb carbon dioxide emissions.

someday moving their families to a safe place keeps the students focused on their studies. "That's what helps me to keep going," says one KANI student, Tiibea Baure. She adds that she is determined "to endure to the end, so that I can bring over my family. I don't want them to die when the land sinks."

Still, some Pacific Islanders resist the idea of leaving. The connection to their homeland is strong. "They talk about us moving. But we are tied to this land," said an inhabitant of the Solomon Islands. "Will we take our cemeteries with us? For we are nothing without our land and our ancestors."

CHAPTER 3
DISASTER IN THE DESERT

IN A REFUGEE CAMP IN THE WEST AFRICAN COUNTRY OF BURKINA FASO, A MAN SITS INSIDE A GRASS HUT. His name is Mohammed, and he comes from the neighboring country of Mali. Both countries belong to a geographic region of north central Africa known as the Sahel. Mohammed tells how he ended up at the refugee camp. "I crossed the border with my animals, my donkeys, my children, and my wife. I traveled to Timbuktu [a city in Mali], crossed the river, and came down to Burkina [Faso]. I walked every day until sunset and after I would go to bed. The journey took three months."

The Sahel is a vast area of grassland speckled with shrubs and stunted trees. It stretches across parts of Senegal, Mauritania, and Mali in the west, all the way across the continent to Sudan and Eritrea on Africa's east coast. To the north lies the Sahara, and to the south is the lush, green savanna (grassland). Home to nearly 100 million people, the Sahel is one of the most unstable regions in the world, plagued by food insecurity, extreme poverty, and war. The majority of people live on less than two dollars a day and struggle to afford food. An estimated 1.4 million children are malnourished. More than half a million children under the age of five die from malnutrition and related causes every year. The region also has the fastest population growth on the planet: 2.8 percent a year, more than twice the global average of 1.2 percent. At this rate of growth, the region will double its population by 2040. With so many people competing for scarce resources, violent conflicts break out frequently. The Sahel's harsh climate is at the root of many of these problems. The region is hot and semiarid, with just two seasons: a short rainy season and a long dry season. It has a stretch of up to ten months with little or no rain.

Migrants displaced by drought and crop failures arrive at a bus station in Maradi, Niger. Water and food shortages plague the Sahel region of Africa, worsening political conflicts and driving millions of people from their homes.

Some people farm, harvesting crops of grains—such as millet, maize, rice, and sorghum—and beans to feed their families. Those near lakes and rivers often fish for a living. Many residents of the Sahel are nomadic cattle herders who move with their herds according to seasonal shifts, following the traditional way of life of their ancestors. All depend on the short rainy season to refill lakes and rivers and to irrigate crops.

Migration is a way of life in the Sahel. Herders graze their herds of cattle, goats, and sheep in the north during the wet season and move south to greener lands in the dry season. During the dry season, many men leave for months to work in large towns or cities. Moving around is a powerful strategy for coping with the harsh environment. But as the region's climate grows hotter and more volatile, the land is less able to support human and animal life. The nomadic life has taken on new urgency as climate change drives people farther and farther from their home territories, often permanently.

Drought and Poverty

In the Sahel, droughts are a regular feature of the environment. In recent years, a climate shift has increased the effects of the recurring droughts. Beginning in the 1960s, the rainy season began to arrive later than usual and leave earlier. Climatologists have linked the dry spell with rising temperatures at the surface of the Indian Ocean, on Africa's east coast. The pattern persisted for decades, creating a long-term shift to a drier climate. This change, combined with human activities such as cutting trees for fuel and new croplands, severely damaged the land. Without trees to hold soil in place, combined with strong regional winds and less overall rainfall, fertile land turned into a dusty desert in a process called desertification. Herders struggled to find fertile pasture for their herds. Farmers waited for the rain, but when it came, it was rarely enough. The harsher climate kicked off a famine. Between the late

1960s and the early 1980s, at least one hundred thousand people and millions of cattle died.

Although the prolonged dry period ended in the 1990s, the land remains deeply damaged, and climate change continues to take a toll. The Sahel is growing steadily hotter. From 1970 to 2006, the average temperature across the region rose by approximately 1.8°F (1°C). The IPCC projects that the region will continue to heat up faster than the global average, with temperatures in West Africa expected to rise 5.4°F to 10.8°F (3°C to 6°C) above temperatures of the late twentieth century. Hotter temperatures can kill vital crops and weaken harvests, which can lead to more food shortages and more famines.

Moreover, the pattern of rainfall is increasingly unpredictable. In the long term, scientists are uncertain whether the region as a whole will become drier or wetter due to climate change. Some fear the Sahel

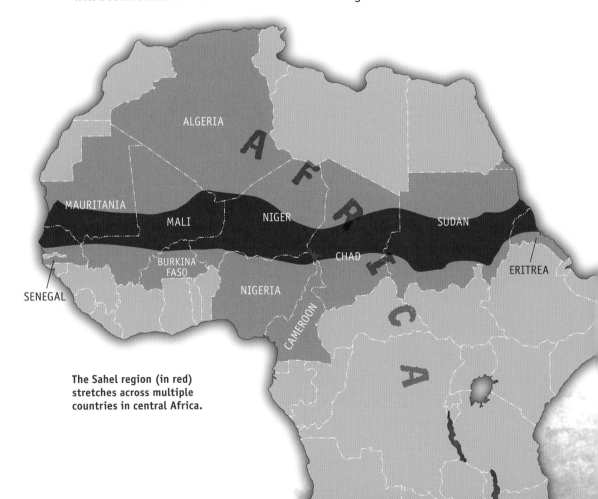

The Sahel region (in red) stretches across multiple countries in central Africa.

could be slammed with more highs and lows—periods of drought followed by devastating floods. After months without precipitation, rain often arrives too early or too late in the growing season to help crops, or it falls in a torrent, causing devastating floods.

Major droughts struck the Sahel in 2005, 2010, and 2012, leading to poor harvests and soaring food prices. During the 2012 crisis, eighteen million people, including one million children, were in danger of starvation. In that same year, severe flooding in the region caused more than seven million people to flee their homes. In 2008 Jan Egeland toured the region as special adviser to the UN secretary-general. He noted the connection between these extreme seasonal cycles and the region's food crises: "People plant seedlings when the rain is supposed to start and then there is nothing, or very little rain, so the seedlings dry up and die. And then suddenly there is this massive rain that comes as a flood and everything is washed away."

Residents of Mauritania use a traditional farming technique called *zai*, digging pits to catch and store rainwater. Unpredictable rainfall has led to long dry periods in Africa's Sahel region, creating challenges for farming families.

Repeated shocks such as these contribute to the region's chronic vulnerability. Families may not be able to grow enough food to make it through the year. When they run out of food from their harvest before new crops are ready, they may be forced to sell their animals, property, and possessions to buy food. "I am losing animals every year," said Barry, a farmer and herder in Burkina Faso, in 2015. He depends on keeping a certain number of animals so that they can breed and replenish his herd over time. "During the difficult months I have to sell a couple to feed my family. Without help there will soon be nothing left."

Even if the next growing season is better, families may not recover. One man, who had sold off his livestock to buy food for his family, said that it would take him at least a year to save up enough money to afford even one new cow. Poor families grow poorer with each passing year, unable to recover from repeated losses.

Fishing families are no better off than farmers and herders. In some areas, lake water has evaporated, transforming lakes into parched desert. This change is caused partly by drought and partly by human overuse of water for farming. When lakes dry up, people are either forced to abandon their livelihood of fishing or move to other lakes—making the region's remaining lakes hot spots for migrants. More than ten thousand people have migrated to Burkina Faso's Lake Bagre since 1994. It is now the most densely populated area in the country, with more people arriving each year.

Most residents of the Sahel are too poor to move to countries that might offer them higher wages or better opportunities. People generally move within their country, but they cross borders if they feel they must. Many abandon their farms and villages and crowd into cities. Herders may search for more fertile pastureland to the south, although this brings them into agricultural areas where farmers grow their crops. Farmers in turn may expand their croplands into areas traditionally used by herders. These movements create tension and conflict over limited lands, food sources, and water.

California Dry Spell

The Sahel isn't the only place where drought and desertification threaten to spark a wave of climate migration. Scientists say climate projections reveal a similar future for the Southwest region of the United States, where severe dry spells and extreme heat are becoming increasingly common. In the state of California, a multiyear drought began in 2012, leading to wildfires, agricultural losses, and severely depleted water supplies. Although the drought began as a natural weather variation, scientists found that climate change dangerously intensified the dry conditions. Increasingly warm temperatures caused more and more water to evaporate from the soil, turning the ground even drier. If heat waves, wildfires, and water shortages become the norm throughout the region, experts say people are likely to flee to cooler, wetter places. According to climatologist Michael E. Mann, "If the drought in California becomes the new normal, and there's a very real

Drought in California

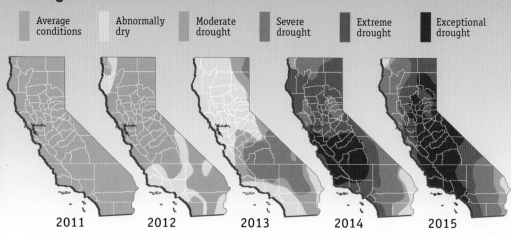

Average conditions   Abnormally dry   Moderate drought   Severe drought   Extreme drought   Exceptional drought

2011   2012   2013   2014   2015

possibility that it does, then we are going to see people driven from their communities, driven from that state. [California] will not be able to meet the water needs of its population if we continue on this course that we're on."

Lynn Wilson, a member of the United Nations' climate change delegation, agrees with that assessment. "Civilizations in the past have had to migrate out of areas of drought," she pointed out in 2014. "We may have to migrate people out of California."

Climate Change in California

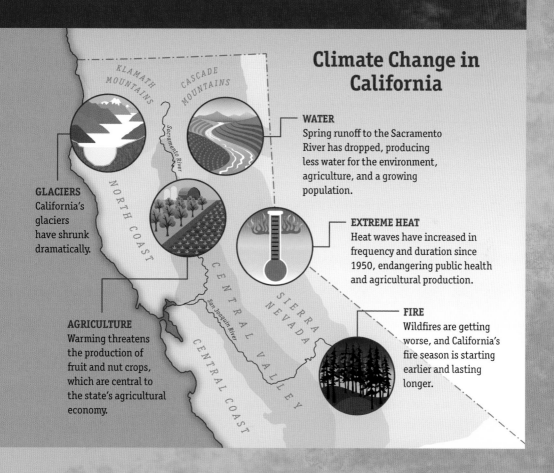

KLAMATH MOUNTAINS

CASCADE MOUNTAINS

Sacramento River

NORTH COAST

CENTRAL VALLEY

San Joaquin River

SIERRA NEVADA

CENTRAL COAST

GLACIERS
California's glaciers have shrunk dramatically.

AGRICULTURE
Warming threatens the production of fruit and nut crops, which are central to the state's agricultural economy.

WATER
Spring runoff to the Sacramento River has dropped, producing less water for the environment, agriculture, and a growing population.

EXTREME HEAT
Heat waves have increased in frequency and duration since 1950, endangering public health and agricultural production.

FIRE
Wildfires are getting worse, and California's fire season is starting earlier and lasting longer.

A Region on the Move

As of 2015, 2.8 million people across the Sahel had been displaced. While no one knows what percentage of them migrated specifically because of climate-related conditions (rather than due to related issues, such as violent conflict), the number of migrants spikes during times of climate crises, such as droughts. Experts predict the number of climate migrants from the region could eventually climb into the tens of millions. "Up to now these people were displaced essentially by conflict," notes Michel Gabaudan, president of the humanitarian, nonprofit organization Refugees International. "But we've seen over the last decade that an increasing number of people are displaced in very large number by climate-related disasters."

Clare Spurrell of the Internal Displacement Monitoring Centre explains that climate change worsens the region's other problems. "Here, vulnerability to disaster triggered by floods is frequently further compounded by hunger, poverty, and violence," she notes, "resulting in a 'perfect storm' of risk factors that lead to displacement." These crises are likely to continue as regional temperatures keep climbing and rainfall remains unreliable.

The poorest and most vulnerable people often have the most difficulty moving. In times of drought and climbing food prices, people spend more of their limited money on food, leaving less available to cover the expenses of transportation and new housing. Many people move step by step, drifting increasingly farther from their original homes as they search for an environment that will support them. New arrivals strain the resources of poor rural villages. Eventually both newcomers and long-term residents move on, looking for a more sustainable life elsewhere. Some people abandon their efforts to live off the land altogether and crowd into nearby cities to look for jobs. Those who can't find work turn to begging. Many rural people who have moved to the Sahel's towns and cities long to return to their traditional ways of life. One man, a herder who moved to the town of Abalak in northern Niger after losing his entire herd in the 2005 drought, asked, "What business does a herder have in town?"

Too Hot for Humans

By the end of this century, the Persian Gulf region of the Middle East could see waves of heat and humidity so severe that being outside for a few hours could endanger human life. In a study published by Loyola Marymount University and Massachusetts Institute of Technology (MIT) in 2015, researchers studied regional forecasts for the Persian Gulf based on current emissions trends. The study's authors found that lethal summertime combinations of heat and humidity could become common in Persian Gulf cities by century's end. These conditions would not be the norm in the region, but deadly waves of muggy weather would become increasingly frequent. "If people in these cities remain in an air-conditioned environment [during a severe heat spike], then they will be safe," notes Elfatih Eltahir, a coauthor of the study. While access to air-conditioning is widespread in wealthier parts of the region, especially cities, it is far less common among people in poorer areas. Ordinary outdoor activities, such as farm labor or even traditional outdoor prayers for Muslim pilgrims, would also pose great health risks during extreme heat outbreaks. The study's authors believe that reducing global greenhouse gas emissions could prevent these extreme heat waves.

Solutions for the Sahel

Countries in the Sahel have a reputation for being generous hosts to refugees. Yet a large influx of people could strain their capacities as they deal with climate changes of their own. As early as 2012, Alice Thomas of Refugees International noted the burden on host communities, especially poor villages already facing shortages of food and water: "Are you going to see local communities getting less patient with the resources being spent on refugees?" Even in the region's cities, jobs and affordable housing are scarce, forcing many migrants to live in slums. Humanitarian organizations urge governments to adopt policies that make relocation easier, safer, and more affordable for struggling families. Advocates also say that simply allowing people to move is not enough. Migrants will need help adjusting to their new homes: finding housing, gaining employment, and accessing public services such as health care and education.

Meanwhile, resilience measures can help people remain on the land for as long as possible. Since the 1960s, the United States and Europe have delivered food and other humanitarian aid to the region in times of extreme stress. This emergency relief has saved the lives of millions of people. In the future, humanitarian aid organizations say that emergency aid can prevent climate shocks from turning into a catastrophe, such as a deadly famine.

But emergency aid is not enough, says Thomas. "As these emergencies are coming closer and closer together, it becomes more and more important that you can build resilience that is actually effective," she explains. Experts say the most promising strategies for adapting to climate change involve community members in the decision making and incorporate residents' knowledge, skills, and strategies for living off the land.

For example, farmers in the western Sahel have had great success with agroforestry, the practice of nurturing and protecting trees that grow naturally among their crops. The trees offer shade and relief from the heat, and they help block wind-blown sand that can bury crops. Fallen tree leaves help enrich the soil, making it more fertile for growing crops. Pruning and selling branches for firewood gives farmers a valuable source of income.

"Twenty years ago, after the drought, our situation here was quite desperate," said Salif Ali, a farmer in Mali who practices agroforestry. "But now we live much better. Before, most families had only one granary [grain storehouse] each. Now, they have three or four, though the land they cultivate has not increased. And we have more livestock as well." Agroforestry has spread rapidly throughout the region. In some parts of the Sahel, nearly all farmers follow the practice, greatly improving their ability to live off the land.

Other options include scientific advances, such as drought-resistant seeds, systems for composting so that farmers can make their own organic fertilizers, improved systems for capturing rainwater, and stone ridges for controlling erosion. Scientists say that farmers and herders become more resilient when they can diversify their livelihood by combining livestock with farming or by growing a mix of crops. Yet putting these advances into practice requires the participation of professionals with technical skills who can train farmers. Progress also depends on support from local institutions and governments. The region's poverty and political instability often present obstacles.

Even with resilience measures in place, migration in the Sahel is likely to continue. As hotter, drought-plagued climates around the world become less able to support human populations, similar patterns of movement may become the norm. Physicist and climate expert Joseph Romm stated in 2012, "Human adaptation to prolonged, extreme drought is difficult or impossible. Historically, the primary adaptation to [drought and desertification] has been abandonment." Dealing with the risks these changes pose to billions of people, he says, "may well be the greatest challenge the human race has ever faced."

Beginning in 2013, farmers in Daga Birame, a village in Senegal, have been adapting their agricultural practices in response to climate change. Residents created a community program to train farmers—such as the woman shown in this photo—to grow drought-resistant, fruit-bearing crops. The program has improved harvests and boosted the village's economy.

CHAPTER 4
COASTS IN CRISIS

ON THE NIGHT OF OCTOBER 29, 2012, HURRICANE SANDY MADE LANDFALL JUST SOUTH OF ATLANTIC CITY, NEW JERSEY. Over the next two days, the storm killed 159 people and caused an estimated $65 billion in damage. It toppled trees, flooded streets, piled up boats in harbors, washed away beaches, filled backyards with debris, and buried streets in sand. The storm damaged or destroyed 650,000 homes, sweeping some of them right off their foundations. As many as 776,000 residents were evacuated from the storm's path. A year later, at least 22,000 households were still displaced, with many dependent on dwindling government relief funds. Those displaced from low-income housing found it especially difficult to return, partly because of moving expenses and partly because the area did not have enough affordable housing. For example, some damaged apartment buildings weren't rebuilt. For others that were rebuilt, landlords charged higher rents than the original residents could afford.

Hurricane Sandy was the second-costliest storm in the country's history. The record holder is Hurricane Katrina, which struck the

United States's southern coast on August 29, 2005. Katrina's storm surge (the bulge of high water that is pushed ashore by wind, waves, and the low pressure of the storm) caused destruction on an enormous scale. Along a 20-mile (32 km) stretch of Mississippi shoreline, the storm surge was a whopping 24 to 28 feet (7.3 to 8.5 m) and penetrated up to 12 miles (19 km) inland along bays and rivers. In New Orleans, where the storm surge reached as high as 19 feet (6 m), water poured over levees and floodwalls designed to protect the

When Hurricane Sandy struck the Northeast coast in October 2012, the storm damaged or destroyed hundreds of thousands of homes, including this one in Union Beach, New Jersey. A year after the storm, thousands of Americans remained displaced.

city, flooding about 80 percent of New Orleans. The storm flattened homes and caused the evacuation of more than one million residents, who fled to cities and towns all over the country. While some were able to return home after a few days or weeks, more than four hundred thousand people were displaced permanently. Studies show that a year after Hurricane Katrina, 53 percent of displaced people had returned to New Orleans, although fewer than one-third were back in their former homes. Of those who stayed away, 12 percent were living elsewhere in Louisiana, while roughly 40 percent were living in the neighboring state of Texas. The rest were scattered around the country.

Terrence Veal is one New Orleans resident who chose not to return. Before Hurricane Katrina made landfall, he left his childhood

Hurricane Katrina, the most expensive storm in the history of the United States, triggered the evacuation of more than one million people from New Orleans, Louisiana, in 2005. More than twenty-five thousand displaced residents temporarily took shelter in the Astrodome stadium in Houston, Texas.

home with his wife, six children, and their belongings all piled in the family car. They ended up in Houston, Texas, with other family members and squeezed twenty-three people into a two-bedroom apartment. "When we came here, we didn't have any money," said Veal. "And we didn't want to put all our children in a shelter because it was just too much moving that we had to do. And so we came together as a family and rented an apartment." Veal said the move allowed him to make a fresh start. He returned to school, earned a master's degree in education, and is studying for his teacher's certification exam. Veal and his family have since settled into a suburban home in Houston.

Thousands of others had less success in finding permanent housing in the years after Katrina. For a few years, the Federal Emergency Management Agency (FEMA) provided temporary housing for displaced survivors. But many low-income people were unable to afford permanent homes after the FEMA aid ended. Vulnerable survivors are especially likely to struggle with long-term displacement. For instance, a 2014 study of displaced low-income African American mothers from New Orleans found that those who couldn't move back to the city faced significantly more emotional strain than those who did return. For many, the words of displaced New Orleans resident Carol Young still ring true. In 2006 Young told an interviewer, "I wish I could go back [to New Orleans], but I know it's impossible. Many days and nights I sit up in this apartment and I have cried. My whole life has been rooted up and I have been put somewhere else, somewhere I didn't ask to be at."

Survivors of Sandy and Katrina are unlikely to be the only Americans permanently displaced by coastal storms. According to one study, for every 1.8°F (1°C) rise in global average surface temperature, the chance of a Katrina-size storm—as measured by the height of the storm surge—could rise two- to sevenfold. Combined with a possible three-foot (1 m) rise in sea level in the twenty-first century, that increase will make coastal areas in the United States and around the world significantly more vulnerable

In the Path of Rising Seas

Worldwide, waves of climate migrants are fleeing coastal cities, where more damaging storms are only part of the problem. Even without the threat of hurricanes, rising sea levels cause frequent flooding and threaten to submerge some areas completely. In the Netherlands, two-thirds of the population already lives below sea level. Other European countries that will be significantly affected by sea level rise include Germany, France, Belgium, Denmark, Spain, and Italy. Half of Asia's urban population lives in low-lying danger zones. In Bangladesh, China, and Vietnam, heavily populated coasts are already under siege from rising seas and could be submerged by the end of the century. These changes will displace large numbers of people. In one scientific study published in 2011, researchers calculated that a 1.6-foot (0.5 m) sea level rise—on the low end of what the IPCC predicts for this century—would displace 72 million people worldwide. A 6.5-foot (2 m) rise, which evidence suggests is possible, would displace 187 million people—more than 2 percent of the world's population.

According to a 2016 study, a three-foot sea level rise could put more than 4 million people in the United States at risk. A 2011 study considered the possible effects on four low-lying, flood-prone areas—Northern California, the state of New Jersey, the state of South Carolina, and southern Florida. If seas rise 1.6 to 5.5 inches (4.2 to 14 cm) by 2030, twenty million people in those four areas alone could be at risk. In Northern California, in densely settled counties around Sacramento, the state's capital, flooding would inundate valuable farmland and small towns. Northeastern New Jersey, a heavily populated coastal region that is officially part of greater New York City, is particularly vulnerable to hurricanes and storm surges. In fact, the region experienced some of the highest and most damaging storm surges during Hurricane Sandy. As seawater rises along the low-lying South Carolina coast, barrier islands are being washed away, leaving communities exposed to more storm impact and damage. In addition to the threats of

The annual rainy monsoon season in Bangladesh causes severe flooding in many parts of the low-lying South Asian nation. This road in the capital city of Dhaka flooded after massive rains in the summer of 2014. More than one million people were displaced by the monsoon.

hurricanes, storm surges, and flooding, saltwater intrusion into drinking water supplies could pose a public health threat.

Tellingly, most of these areas have vulnerable populations. South Florida is home to millions of retirees, who may be financially or physically unable to relocate. Many residents of Northern California and coastal South Carolina live in poverty. Relocation and recovery after displacement can be especially challenging for poor people. They have less money than wealthy people, and they tend to have fewer job skills and fewer opportunities for work.

Adapting in Bangladesh

In 2012 Ajmad Miyah lost everything he owned when the rising sea destroyed his farm on the coast of Bangladesh, a South Asian nation of about 160 million people. Three years later, he was scraping by as a field hand, laboring on other people's farms. "I've accepted that this is my reality," he said in 2015. "My house will always be temporary now, like me on this earth."

The poor, low-lying nation of Bangladesh has been called "the most climate vulnerable country in the world." Bordered on the south by the Bay of Bengal, Bangladesh is at high risk from extreme storms, floods, and the spread of salt water, which contaminates drinking water and kills crops. As sea levels rise over the twenty-first century, up to 20 percent of the country's land area could disappear, and at least fifteen million people could be displaced.

In response to these dire predictions, the country has focused on raising awareness about climate change and shoring up its defenses, often with funding from international donors such as the United Nations. Local people are busy building and strengthening embankments, designing and erecting disaster-resilient homes, and planting salt-resistant crops. Despite being one of the poorest countries in the world, Bangladesh has become a global leader in climate adaptation, drawing on widespread public support to implement grassroots projects.

Villagers in coastal Bangladesh rebuild a protective embankment damaged by Cyclone Aila in 2009. These women use mud to strengthen the damaged stone barrier against the sea.

Following Hurricane Katrina, homelessness rates soared in New Orleans and the surrounding area. In 2012, seven years after the storm, about forty-nine hundred New Orleans residents—more than twice the pre-Katrina number—were homeless. This January 2014 photo shows Larry Nunn Sr., a homeless New Orleans resident.

While some cities are pledging to make their cities more resilient, many communities are ill-prepared to deal with the effects of climate change. In fact, New Orleans may be one of these cities. Since Hurricane Katrina, the federal government has worked with city and state leaders to strengthen the city's levees and to revise evacuation plans and emergency procedures. But critics say most of the emphasis has been on how to evacuate people safely, rather than on how to ease recovery afterward. "Getting residents out is certainly important; doing it right will save lives and simplify efforts to restore critical services," acknowledges Stephen Flynn, the president of the Center for National Policy, an independent policy institute in Washington, DC. "But if there are no plans for what comes next, many people may not return."

CHAPTER 5
THE FUTURE OF CLIMATE MIGRATION

THE YEAR 2015 WAS THE HOTTEST ON RECORD FOR THE PLANET. Climatologists don't believe the year's unprecedented average global temperature was a fluke. By 2015 thirteen of the hottest years on record had occurred since 2000. The odds of that happening by chance alone—without the boost of climate change—are one in twenty-seven million.

Experts often compare climate change to a speeding train. The train has so much momentum that even slamming on the brakes won't instantly bring it to a halt. In the same way, if humans stopped burning fossil fuels right now, the climate would keep warming. Greenhouse gases already in the air will linger in the atmosphere for decades or centuries, warming the climate for years to come. By releasing greenhouse gases to the air, humans have committed Earth to decades, even centuries, of warming.

As the planet heats up, people in developing countries, low-lying islands, and coastal areas are being affected first. Worldwide, the number of people retreating from natural disasters and climate change is already rising. In 2014 natural disasters drove nineteen million people from their homes. Most of these people lived in Asia and were fleeing floods and typhoons. (A typhoon is the same type of strong tropical storm as a hurricane. A storm that forms over the northwestern Pacific Ocean is called a typhoon, while a storm that forms over the Atlantic or Northeast Pacific is called a hurricane. A storm that forms over the southern Pacific Ocean or the Indian Ocean is called a cyclone.)

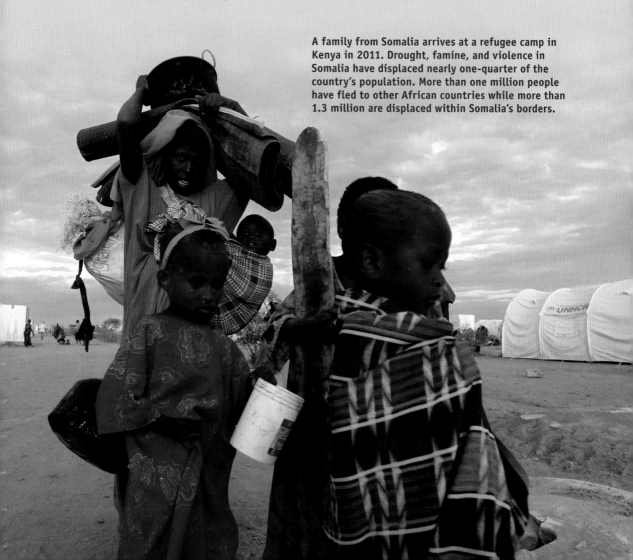

A family from Somalia arrives at a refugee camp in Kenya in 2011. Drought, famine, and violence in Somalia have displaced nearly one-quarter of the country's population. More than one million people have fled to other African countries while more than 1.3 million are displaced within Somalia's borders.

Most experts agree that by 2050, at least twenty-five million people—roughly the population of Texas—will be climate migrants. Some think that if emissions continue unchecked, up to one billion people could be forced to move. That number is roughly equal to the populations of North America and Europe combined. The difference between those low and high estimates reflects a general uncertainty about the scope of the problem. No one knows precisely how many people will be driven from their homes. The scale of migration will be determined by future events. For instance, if officials in a low-lying coastal city take measures to protect city residents, then fewer people will have to move. If city officials fail to act, people will be forced to retreat.

Future greenhouse gas emissions are probably the biggest factor in the uncertainty. Reducing emissions may reduce the magnitude of warming. This in turn will cut down on how many people ultimately are forced to move. The actions that the world takes in the next few decades will determine how many people are driven from their homes by climate change.

Business as Usual

When climate scientists talk about what the future might look like if global emissions continue to grow unchecked, they use the term *business as usual*. Under business as usual, the planet's average temperature is expected to climb 5.7°F to 9.7°F (3.2°C to 5.4°C) above preindustrial temperatures by the end of the century. Many scientists agree that anything more than a global average of 3.6°F (2°C) of warming above preindustrial levels would trigger irreversibly dangerous levels of climate change. Global climate action is aimed at keeping warming below this threshold. Some experts argue that even this theoretical limit would be too much warming and would place large numbers of people in danger. In any case, if emissions stay on the business-as-usual track, the global average temperature increase will surpass 3.6°F within the next thirty years.

Scientists, activists, and political leaders debate whether the world will be able to stop the warming at or below 3.6°F (2°C). "People are saying either 'It's already a little late to hold it to two degrees [Celsius]' or 'We'd have to work really, really hard to hold it to two degrees,'" says climate scientist Richard Alley. "Some people say 'Nah, we can still do it.'" He points out that as global temperature rise, the dangers for people and the environment escalate. "As you go to three, four, five [degrees Celsius], the costs go up really fast."

Preventing a Crisis

Humans cannot stop climate change, but they can slow it and protect the planet from at least some of its devastating effects. Studies clearly show that with effective climate policies and the use of existing technologies, the world can substantially lower global emissions, slow climate change, and significantly reduce the ultimate number of climate migrants. These steps would not reverse the warming that is already occurring. But a combination of strategies, each helping to reduce rising global emissions, could get the world on a path to stabilizing the climate. "There's no silver bullet," says Ray Najjar, a professor of oceanography at Pennsylvania State University who studies climate change. "But there are a lot of small things we can do that add up to a solution."

The most effective way to fight climate change is to use less energy. On an individual level, this can involve making lifestyle changes. For instance, burning 1 gallon (3.8 liters) of gasoline releases nearly 20 pounds (9 kg) of carbon dioxide into the atmosphere. Biking, walking, or taking a bus or a train uses far less energy than traveling by petroleum-powered car. Recycling saves energy because it reduces the energy needed to make materials from scratch. Americans can turn off lights to save energy because most electricity in the United States is generated by burning coal or natural gas. These kinds of measures can add up to significant emission cuts if millions of people commit to them in their daily lives.

The Great Green Wall

In the Sahel and Sahara regions of Africa, people are hard at work on the Great Green Wall, an ambitious project funded by the World Bank, the African Union, the United Nations, and individual countries. The goal of the project is to halt desertification by creating a belt of restored land—a mosaic of forests, shrubs, grasslands, and sustainable farmland—across the African continent. At 4,400 miles (7,100 km) long and 9 miles (15 km) wide, the belt would run through eleven African countries—Djibouti, Eritrea, Ethiopia, Sudan, Chad, Niger, Nigeria, Mali, Burkina Faso, Mauritania, and Senegal.

The country that has made the most progress on the Great Green Wall is Senegal. Every year since 2008, hundreds of people have planted two million native trees. Papa Sarr, technical director for the Great Green Wall in Senegal, notes that project managers choose these trees carefully. "When we design a parcel, we look at the local trees and see what can best grow there, we try to copy nature," he explained in 2014. In addition to being able to survive in the hot, dry conditions, some trees are chosen for the valuable products they give. For instance, several species of acacia trees produce gum arabic, a substance used in many foods, cosmetics, and pharmaceutical products.

Matar Cisse, director of Senegal's Great Green Wall project, holds gum arabic produced by acacia trees.

At its core, the Great Green Wall is about improving the land. Plants keep soil from blowing away, help rainwater filter into the ground, and provide habitats for animals. They also serve as carbon sinks, trapping carbon dioxide and removing it from the air, helping to offset climate change. Ultimately, those involved in the project hope to boost the region's food security, alleviate poverty, and help communities adapt to climate change.

Using less energy can also mean improving energy efficiency—minimizing energy that is lost or wasted. People do this on a small scale by using energy-efficient lighting, appliances, and electronic devices in homes and businesses. On a larger scale, automobile companies can make more fuel-efficient cars. In 2012 President Obama worked to tighten fuel economy standards for cars and trucks. The new, higher standards will reduce greenhouse gas emissions in the United States, while saving consumers money in gasoline.

Another strategy to combat climate change is to use energy in ways that will not emit carbon dioxide in the first place. One method, called carbon capture and storage, or CCS, traps carbon dioxide from a power plant or other source of pollution before it is released into the atmosphere. Carbon dioxide is filtered out from the mix of gases produced during fossil fuel combustion. Trucks, ships, and pipelines then transport that carbon dioxide to a storage site, where it is injected into cracks in porous rocks deep under the ground. Carbon capture has problems that have limited its use. It uses energy and is expensive to implement. Captured carbon must be stored safely without risk of leaking to the surface. Leakage can be dangerous.

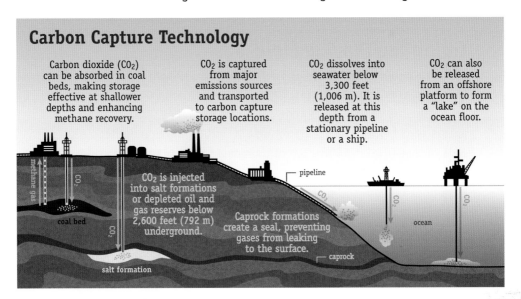

Carbon Capture Technology

Carbon dioxide (CO_2) can be absorbed in coal beds, making storage effective at shallower depths and enhancing methane recovery.

CO_2 is captured from major emissions sources and transported to carbon capture storage locations.

CO_2 dissolves into seawater below 3,300 feet (1,006 m). It is released at this depth from a stationary pipeline or a ship.

CO_2 can also be released from an offshore platform to form a "lake" on the ocean floor.

CO_2 is injected into salt formations or depleted oil and gas reserves below 2,600 feet (792 m) underground.

Caprock formations create a seal, preventing gases from leaking to the surface.

methane gas

coal bed

salt formation

pipeline

caprock

ocean

This illustration shows how carbon capture technology prevents carbon dioxide emissions from escaping into the atmosphere.

Carbon dioxide normally mixes into the air, but a large leak could create a pocket of unmixed carbon dioxide that could kill people and wildlife in the area.

Transitioning from fossil fuels to renewable sources of energy can also reduce carbon dioxide emissions. Unlike fossil fuels, renewable energy sources—such as solar power, wind power, and hydropower—will never run out. Most emit no greenhouse gases (though some greenhouse gases are emitted in the initial production of equipment such as solar panels and wind turbines and in the building of infrastructure such as dams). As concerns about climate change grow, use of alternative energy is increasing. In 2014 renewable energy sources accounted for about 13 percent of electricity generated in the United States, up from 9 percent a decade earlier. Alternative energy remains more expensive than fossil fuels. This is partly because many countries, including the United States, give sums of money called subsidies to fossil fuel companies. By shifting some subsidies from fossil fuels to alternative energy, governments could create a boom in investment in alternative energies, bring down their cost, and ultimately bring down carbon emissions.

Tilting the Playing Field

Climate change is not only an environmental problem but an economic one. Floods, storms, forced migration, and other consequences of climate change cost a lot of money. "Each of the 35 billion tons [31.8 billion metric tons] of carbon dioxide emitted *this year* causes at least $40 worth of damages to the planet, possibly much more," write Gernot Wagner and Martin L. Weitzman in their 2015 book *Climate Shock: The Economic Consequences of a Hotter Planet.* That adds up to $1.4 trillion of damage in just one year. Some economists set the price higher or lower. But they generally agree that the damage from climate change is costly.

Despite these long-term costs, fossil fuels are cheaper to produce and to purchase than alternative energy sources. Economists have outlined two different approaches to making polluters pay for the damage they create from carbon dioxide. One is a carbon tax, which would raise the cost of fossil fuels as well as the cost of products and services that use a lot of fossil fuels. Such a tax would give consumers a powerful incentive to conserve energy and switch to alternative sources of energy, which would not be taxed. Countries that have instituted some form of a carbon tax include India, Costa Rica, South Africa, and Canada.

A cap-and-trade system takes a different approach, in which countries place a limit or cap on the overall carbon emissions allowed in each country. Countries are given credits that allow them to emit a certain amount of carbon. For example, if a nation currently emits 40 million tons (36 million metric tons) of carbon and its goal is to cut emissions by 25 percent, then that nation would receive permits to emit 30 million tons (27 million metric tons) of carbon. Permits could then be auctioned off to power plants, factories, and suppliers of fossil fuels. Companies that managed to lower their emissions could sell their extra permits to other companies. If a company chooses to use alternative, noncarbon energy sources, it could sell its extra permits to a high-emitting company. Environmental groups could purchase permits and permanently retire them—meaning they won't actually produce the emissions they've paid for and won't resell the rights to anyone else—thus bringing down overall emissions.

Fossil Fuel Divestment

Activists around the world are using divestment to pressure the fossil fuel industry to switch to alternative energies. Divestment is getting rid of stocks, bonds, and other investments in companies that the investor considers unethical. The campaign has spread to more than forty countries. As of September 2015, four hundred institutions—including universities, pension funds, and churches—and at least two thousand individuals had divested a total of $2.6 trillion from coal, oil, and gas companies.

The European Union set up a cap-and-trade system for carbon in 2005, and that program has helped lower greenhouse gas emissions. In 2015 President Barack Obama announced a national cap-and-trade plan that requires US power plants to slash emissions to 68 percent of their 2005 levels by 2030. With either a carbon tax or a cap-and-trade system, "polluters pay when they are doing the polluting and, hence, will pollute less," say Wagner and Weitzman.

A Global Action Plan

Political leaders disagree about which countries should cut emissions and by how much. Although the world's industrialized countries have high emissions compared to the rest of the world, most of the growth in emissions is in developing countries. Developing countries argue that they should not have to limit their emissions when industrialized countries emit so much more. At the same time, industrialized countries are reluctant to limit emissions because they believe it will be costly, slow their economies, and put them at a disadvantage against developing countries, such as China and India.

This controversy haunted the first global climate pact ever made: the Kyoto Protocol, which was in effect from 2005 through 2012. It required participating industrialized nations, which had caused most of the climate pollution, to reduce their greenhouse gas emissions. Developing nations were not required to take action. The United States refused to even ratify the treaty, and ultimately the agreement had little impact on greenhouse gas emissions. At the next climate talks in Lima, Peru, in 2014, the United States and China—two of the world's biggest greenhouse gas polluters—came to a breakthrough agreement. The United States committed to producing 26 to 28 percent less climate-changing pollution in 2025 than it had in 2005. China agreed to freeze its annual greenhouse gas emission rates by 2030. The European Union stepped forward with its own goals of reducing its greenhouse gas emissions in 2030 by 40 percent compared with 1990.

In 2015 nations finalized the new climate agreement in Paris, France. This accord called for action from all nations, not just wealthy ones, and provided funding for developing countries to reduce emissions and adapt to climate change. Recognizing the effect that climate change will have on mass migration, the Paris accord called for international advisory groups to develop approaches "to avert, minimize and address displacement related to the adverse impacts of climate change." Still, some experts and activists fear this language is too vague to create real change. Marine Franck, chair of an international advisory group on climate change and human mobility,

Displaced Somalians, fleeing a massive drought and the resulting food shortage, wait to enter a refugee camp in Ethiopia in 2011. A global plan to combat climate change aims to help reduce the security of climate-change-fueled droughts like the one in Somalia.

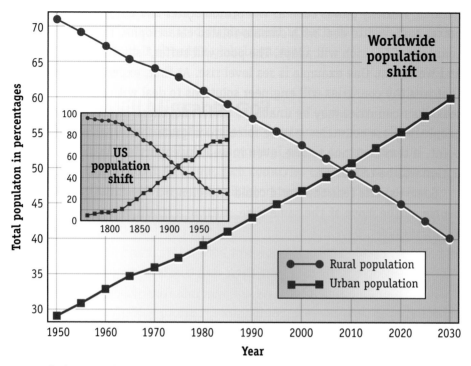

The large graph shows the worldwide global shift from a mostly rural population to a mostly urban one. The US population graph (INSET) mirrors this worldwide trend over a longer period of time. Americans moved from the countryside to cities as the industrial revolution gained momentum.

better access to jobs, health care, and education. It can provide opportunities to use land in a more environmentally friendly way and protect natural ecosystems in areas outside of cities. Most of the world's cities, however, are not equipped to support a large influx of migrants. As people crowd into cities, many are forced to live in cramped, unhealthy living conditions in the poorest neighborhoods. Cities are often unable to provide enough jobs for the newcomers, resulting in high unemployment. Crime can rise as people struggle to afford the costs of their everyday needs. These conditions violate an internationally recognized principle of voluntary resettlement: people must be at least as well off after resettlement as before. Urban areas also tend to be hotter than surrounding rural areas, creating what is known as an urban heat island. Cities contain large expanses of asphalt and other surfaces that hold heat. Trees and other vegetation, which provide shade and create a cooling effect, are in short supply. Close spacing of buildings disrupts wind flow and prevents buildings from releasing their heat back into space at night. High levels of pollution can warm the air. The urban heat island effect, combined with climate change, could lead to scorching temperatures in cities as the twenty-first century progresses.

Resettlement affects not only the people moving but also their host communities. How can migrants settle peacefully among their new neighbors? Host communities themselves will be experiencing climate change and may find themselves threatened by floods, drought, stronger storms, or water scarcity. In a community under stress, with an influx of migrants, tension and conflict can spring up between longtime residents and newcomers. A peaceful and well-organized resettlement must take into account the needs of the citizens of host communities. One way to ease tensions is with inclusive programs that benefit both newcomers and their hosts. For instance, a resettlement plan might offer health, education, and work training programs to climate migrants as well as to people already living in the host communities. Offering the program to all residents—instead of only newcomers—could help ease resentment and animosity from the host community. Inclusive programs would also require extra funding, however.

Many climate migrants must manage as well as they can without such safety nets. Mohammad Ayub Ali left his hometown in central Bangladesh after poor harvests and a massive flood ruined his livelihood. By 2009 he was working as a rickshaw driver in Dhaka. He lived with his mother, wife, and two children in a one-room shack in the city's crowded slums. "It's not that great over here," he acknowledged, referring to the lack of job opportunities and affordable housing, "but it's better than over there [in the devastated countryside]."

Preview of a Global Migration?

To see what life could be like in a world with huge waves of migrants, consider the migrant crisis in Europe in 2015. In that year, huge numbers of migrants—ten thousand people a day at the peak—fled civil wars in Middle Eastern and African countries and made their way to Europe. The wave of migrants brought the total number of displaced people in the world to sixty million, the largest amount since World War II (1939–1945).

Europe's political leaders struggled with how to handle the crisis and quarreled over how many refugees each country should host. While some Europeans welcomed refugees, others protested at anti-immigrant rallies and threw their support behind anti-immigrant political parties.

Although violent conflict has been the main force driving people to flee the Middle East and Africa, climate change is roiling these same societies. One study found that a 2007–2010 drought, caused by climate change, helped fuel a massive political conflict in Syria. "We're not saying the drought caused [the violence]," emphasizes climate scientist Richard Seager. "We're saying that added to all the other stressors, it helped kick things over the threshold into open conflict." By late 2015, more than six million people had been displaced within Syria, and an additional four million had fled to other countries.

Even as European countries take in migrants from other regions, they are experiencing disruptive climate changes of their own. Mediterranean countries such as Italy and Greece are projected to grow hotter and drier in the coming decades. Many of their own citizens may head north to join the ranks of people on the move. Some experts think that as climate change continues, migrant waves on the scale of Europe's recent influx could become the new normal for nations around the world.

Most Syrian refugees spend months or years living in refugee camps with limited resources and often unhealthy conditions. This image shows Syrian children at a camp in Beirut, Lebanon, in November 2015.

Facing the Future

For most climate migrants, displacement is challenging emotionally as well as financially. Anthropologist Anthony Oliver-Smith says, "In forced migration, people lose not only resources and property but also employment and livelihoods, social networks, kin [family], political power, and a sense of meaning and cultural identity." The experience can be especially wrenching for people who must give up traditional means of living and other location-based cultural practices that have been passed down for generations. Ancestral burial grounds, historic landmarks, and beloved landscapes will disappear forever. Migrants and their descendants will feel these emotional impacts long after they relocate.

Yet even in the face of such enormous loss, many people are determined to make the most of their situations. In 2014, faced with the prospect of eventually needing to evacuate their island nation, the government of Kiribati purchased a 12-square-mile (31 sq km) piece of land in the nearby Fiji Islands. "We would hope not to put everyone on [this] one piece of land, but if it became absolutely necessary, yes, we could do it," stated President Anote Tong. This mix of realism and hopefulness is familiar to climate migrants and potential future climate migrants around the world.

To survive and thrive in new settings, climate migrants will need the support of national governments and small communities, international organizations and local businesses. Creative strategies can minimize the number of people who ultimately need to move and can ease the transition for those who do. As climate change alters the landscape of the planet, it will test the resourcefulness and resilience of millions of people across the globe.

Glossary

adaptation: adjustments that a person or a group can make to survive and thrive under certain conditions

agroforestry: a system of agriculture in which trees are grown among crops or pastureland to help prevent soil erosion

alternative energy: energy such as wind power and solar energy that is not generated from fossil fuel sources

asylum: the protection granted by a host country to people who have left their native country as political refugees

atoll: a ring-shaped island or chain of islands made of coral

cap and trade: an environmental policy that involves setting a mandatory limit (or cap) on certain types of pollution and allowing companies to sell (or trade) the unused portion of their limits to other companies

carbon capture and storage: the process of trapping carbon dioxide produced by burning fossil fuels and storing it, preventing it from entering the atmosphere

carbon dioxide: a colorless, odorless gas that traps heat in the atmosphere and contributes to climate change

carbon tax: a tax on the use of fossil fuels based on how much carbon dioxide they emit. The tax is intended to reduce carbon dioxide emissions.

climate change: long-term changes in weather patterns, such as increased numbers of severe storms, floods, droughts, and heat waves

coral reef: a structure in shallow, tropical seas composed of the skeletons of small animals called coral

cyclone: a large storm with violent winds that forms over the South Pacific Ocean or the Indian Ocean

desertification: the process by which fertile land becomes desert, typically through a combination of climate conditions such as drought and human activities

developing country: a country in which the majority of the population lives on less money and with fewer public services than the population of a highly industrialized country

drought: a prolonged period of low rainfall

emissions: the production and discharge of air pollutants

erosion: the process by which soil is worn away by water, wind, or ice

food insecurity: a lack of reliable access to affordable, nutritious food

fossil fuel: a substance such as oil, coal, or natural gas that was formed from the remains of prehistoric plants and trees and that gives off carbon dioxide when burned

glacier: a large, slow-moving mass of ice

greenhouse effect: the natural process by which Earth's atmosphere traps heat from the sun, keeping Earth warm. The large-scale burning of fossil fuels has intensified this process, causing Earth's overall temperatures to rise.

greenhouse gas: a substance, such as carbon dioxide, that traps heat in the atmosphere

high tide: the highest point of ocean waters reached twice a day

hurricane: a large storm with violent winds that forms over the Atlantic Ocean or Northeast Pacific Ocean

ice sheet: a mass of ice that covers the ground in polar regions and forms through the accumulation of snowfall

ice shelf: a thick floating slab of ice that forms over water where a glacier or an ice sheet meets the ocean

industrialized nations: countries with highly developed economies, advanced technology, and well-developed industries, such as manufacturing, construction, and mining

industrial revolution: a rapid development of industry, characterized by the introduction of machines and the development of large-scale industries, that began in Britain in the late eighteenth century and spread to other countries during the nineteenth century,

malnutrition: a condition in which the body lacks vitamins, minerals, and nutrients needed to stay healthy

mitigation: actions that lessen the severity of harmful events or conditions

monsoon: the seasonal wind and heavy rain that occurs in southern Asia in summer

ocean acidification: the decrease of pH of Earth's oceans, caused by the uptake of carbon dioxide from the atmosphere

permafrost: a layer of permanently frozen soil underlying much of the land in the Arctic

refugee: a person who is forced from his or her homeland due to danger, such as a violent conflict or persecution based on race, religion, nationality, or political opinion

saltwater intrusion: the movement of salt water into freshwater supplies, which can lead to contamination of drinking water

sea ice: ice that floats on the ocean's surface

thermal expansion: the tendency of materials and substances to change in area, length, and volume in response to a temperature change

typhoon: a large storm with violent winds that forms over the northwestern Pacific Ocean

Source Notes

11 Douglas Causey, interview with the author, April 28, 2015.

12 Charlie Nakqashuk, "Portraits of Resilience: The Meltdown," Many Strong Voices, accessed July 31, 2015, http://www.manystrongvoices.org/portraits /stories.aspx?id=4056.

15 Suzanne Goldenberg, "One Family's Great Escape," video, *Guardian*, May 13, 2013, http://www.theguardian.com/environment/interactive/2013/may/13 /alaskan-family-newtok-mertarvik.

19   Robin Bronen, interview with the author, May 7, 2015.

16   Ina Bouker and Nia White, interviews with the author, May 6, 2015.

16 Ibid.

16 Ibid.

17 Ibid.

23 Richard Alley, interview with the author, August 12, 2015.

24 Brian Reed, "Climate Change and Faith Collide in Kiribati," *National Public Radio*, February 16, 2011, http://www.npr.org/2011/02/16/133650679 /climate-change-and-faith-collide-in-kiribati.

25 "Ocean Acidification Is Climate Change's 'Equally Evil Twin,' NOAA Chief Says," *HuffPost Green*, last modified September 8, 2012, http://www.huffingtonpost .com/2012/07/09/ocean-acidification-reefs-climate-change_n_1658081.html.

25 Christopher Pala, "Warming May Not Swamp Islands," *Science* 345, no. 6196 (August 1, 2014): p. 497.

26 Ibid.

26 Greg Harman, "Has the Great Climate Change Migration Already Begun?," *Guardian*, September 15, 2014, http://www.theguardian.com/vital-signs /2014/sep/15/climate-change-refugees-un-storms-natural-disasters-sea -levels-environment.

27–28 Jeffrey Goldberg, "Drowning Kiribati," *Bloomberg Business*, November 21, 2013, http://www.bloomberg.com/bw/articles/2013-11-21/kiribati-climate -change-destroys-pacific-island-nation#p3.

28 Anote Tong, "Statement by His Excellency Anote Tong, President of the Republic of Kiribati, The General Debate of the 64th General Assembly," 1–2, United Nations, September 25, 2009, http://www.un.org/en/ga/64 /generaldebate/pdf/KI_en.pdf.

30 Volkelr Boege, "Challenges and Pitfalls of Resettlement Measures: Experiences in the Pacific Region," 32, Center on Migration, Citizenship, and Development, December 2010, https://www.uni-bielefeld.de/tdrc/ag_comcad/downloads /workingpaper_102_boege.pdf.

30 David Morris, "Who Should Pay Climate Change Costs?," *Our World*, January 21, 2013, http://ourworld.unu.edu/en/who-should-pay-climate-change-costs.

31–32 Eve Mahnke, "Climate Migration 'a Complex Problem,'" *Our World*, October 31, 2013, http://ourworld.unu.edu/en/climate-migration-a-complex-problem.

32 Justin Worland, "Meet the President Trying to Save His Island Nation from Climate Change," *Time*, October 9, 2015, http://time.com/4058851/kiribati -cliamte-change.

33 Brian Reed, "Preparing for Sea Level Rise, Islanders Leave Home," *National Public Radio*, June 1, 2011, http://www.npr.org/2011/02/17/133681251 /preparing-for-sea-level-rise-islanders-leave-home.

33 Boege, "Challenges and Pitfalls."

34 "Sahel: Malian Refugees and Hosts Hit Hard by Crises," *Refugees International*, accessed July 9, 2015, http://www.refugeesinternational.org/blog/video /sahel-malian-refugees-and-hosts-hit-hard-crises.

38 Jan Egeland, "Sahel Climate Change Diary—Day 1," *IRIN*, June 2, 2008, http://www.irinnews.org/report/78524/sahel-sahel-climate-change-diary -day-1.

39 "Barry's Story," *YouTube* video, 2:00, posted by "United Nations Office for the Coordination of Humanitarian Affairs," February 11, 2015, https://www .youtube.com/watch?v=BbOEg3z0cJk.

40–41 Harman, "Has the Great Climate Change Migration Already Begun?"

41 Pamela Engel, "UN Expert: We Might Have to Migrate People out of California If Drought Continues," *Business Insider*, August 5, 2014, http://www .businessinsider.com/california-drought-may-mean-people-leave-2014-8.

42 Michel Gabaudan, *Living on the Edge of Disaster: Climate's Human Cost*, video. Refugees International, 2013.

42 John Parnell, "USA Suffers Severe Climate Induced Migration," *Climate Home*, last modified February 15, 2013, http://www.climatechangenews.com/2013 /05/14/usa-suffers-severe-climate-induced-migration.

42 "Livelihood Security: Climate Change, Migration and Conflict in the Sahel," United Nations Environment Programme, 2011, http://www.un.org/en/events /environmentconflictday/pdf/UNEP_Sahel_EN.pdf, 55.

43 Eric Holthaus, "No, Climate Change Won't Make the Persian Gulf 'Uninhabitable,'" *Slate*, October 27, 2015, http://www.slate.com/blogs/future _tense/2015/10/27/climate_change_heat_waves_won_t_make_persian_gulf _uninhabitable.html.

43 "Climate Change, Environmental Degradation, and Migration," European Commission, International Dialogue on Migration, April 16, 2013, http:// ec.europa.eu/clima/policies/adaptation/what/docs/swd_2013_138_en.pdf.

44 Lisa Friedman, "Climate Will Pose Next Threat to Refugees from Fighting and Food Shortages in Mali," *Scientific American*, May 31, 2012, http://www .scientificamerican.com/article/malians-fleeing-drought-famine-war-climate -refugees.

Selected Bibliography

Adams, Sophie, Florent Baarsch, Alberte Bondeau, Dim Coumou, Reik Donner, Katja Frieler, Bill Hare, et al. *Turn Down the Heat: Climate Extremes, Regional Impacts, and the Case for Resilience*. World Bank. June 1, 2013. http://documents .worldbank.org/curated/en/2013/06/17862361/turn-down-heat-climate -extremes-regional-impacts-case-resilience-full-report.

Alley, Richard B. *Earth: The Operator's Manual*. New York: W. W. Norton, 2011.

"A Brief History of the Settlement of Newtok and Village Relocation Efforts." State of Alaska. Accessed April 22, 2015. https://www.commerce. alaska.gov/web/dcra/PlanningLandManagement/NewtokPlanningGroup/ NewtokVillageRelocationHistory.aspx.

Davenport, Coral. "Miami Finds Itself Ankle-Deep in Climate Change Debate." *New York Times*, May 7, 2014. http://www.nytimes.com/2014/05/08/us/florida-finds -itself-in-the-eye-of-the-storm-on-climate-change.html.

Friedman, Lisa. "Climate Will Pose Next Threat to Refugees from Fighting and Food Shortages in Mali." *Scientific American*, May 31, 2012. http://www .scientificamerican.com/article/malians-fleeing-drought-famine-war-climate -refugees.

Goldberg, Jeffrey. "Drowning Kiribati." *Bloomberg Business*, November 21, 2013. http://www.bloomberg.com/bw/articles/2013-11-21/kiribati-climate-change -destroys-pacific-island-nation.

Goldenberg, Suzanne. "America's First Climate Refugees." *Guardian*, May 13, 2013. http://www.theguardian.com/environment/interactive/2013/may/13/newtok -alaska-climate-change-refugees.

Heffernan, Olive. "Adapting to a Warmer World: No Going Back." *Nature* 491, no. 7426 (2012): 659–661. http://www.nature.com/news/adapting-to-a-warmer-world-no -going-back-1.11906.

Hertsgaard, Mark. "The Great Green Wall: African Farmers Beat Back Drought and Climate Change with Trees." *Scientific American*, January 28, 2011. http://www .scientificamerican.com/article/farmers-in-sahel-beat-back-drought-and-climate -change-with-trees.

Intergovernmental Panel on Climate Change. *Climate Change 2014: Impacts, Adaptation, and Vulnerability. Part a: Global and Sectoral Aspects. Contribution of Working Group II to the Fifth Assessment Report of the Intergovernmental Panel on Climate Change*. Edited by Christopher B. Field, V. Barros, D. J. Dokken, K. J. Mach, M. D. Mastrandrea, T. E. Bilir, M. Chatterjee, et al. Cambridge: Cambridge University Press, 2014.

———. *Managing the Risks of Extreme Events and Disasters to Advance Climate Change Adaptation*. Edited by Christopher B. Field, V. Barros, T. F. Stocker, D. Qin, D. J. Dokken, K. L. Ebi, M. D. Mastrandrea, et al. Cambridge: Cambridge University Press, 2012.

International Organization for Migration. "IOM Outlook on Migration, Environment and Climate Change." International Organization for Migration. Geneva: International Organization for Migration, 2014. http://publications.iom.int /bookstore/free/MECC_Outlook.pdf.

Kolbert, Elizabeth. *Field Notes from a Catastrophe: Man, Nature, and Climate Change*. New York: Bloomsbury, 2006.

Melillo, Jerry M., Terese Richmond, and Gary W. Yohe, eds. *Climate Change Impacts in the United States: The Third National Climate Assessment*. US Global Change Research Program, 2014. http://nca2014.globalchange.gov.

"Moving Stories: The Sahel." UK Climate Change and Migration Coalition. (Blog). April 16, 2013. http://climatemigration.org.uk/moving-stories-the-sahel.

National Academy of Sciences. *Arctic Matters: The Global Connection to Changes in the Artic*. Accessed August 3, 2015. http://dels.nas.edu/resources/static-assets /materials-based-on-reports/booklets/ArcticMatters.pdf.

National Research Council. *Abrupt Impacts of Climate Change: Anticipating Surprises*. Washington, DC: National Academies Press, 2013.

Refugees International. *Sahel: Recurrent Climate Shocks Propel Migration; Resilience Efforts Face Challenges*. August 1, 2013. http://www.refworld.org/docid /522052a34.html.

"Stabilization Wedges." Princeton University. Last modified March 10, 2015. http:// cmi.princeton.edu/wedges.

United Nations Environment Programme. *Livelihood Security: Climate Change, Migration and Conflict in the Sahel*. 2011. http://www.un.org/en/events /environmentconflictday/pdf/UNEP_Sahel_EN.pdf.

US Environmental Protection Agency. *Climate Change in the United States: Benefits of Global Action*. EPA. Accessed August 21, 2015. http://www2.epa.gov/cira.

Wagner, Gernot, and Martin L. Weitzman. *Climate Shock: The Economic Consequences of a Hotter Planet*. Princeton, NJ: Princeton University Press, 2015.

Warner, Koko, Charles Ehrhart, Alex de Sherbinin, Susan Adams, and Tricia Chai-Onn. *In Search of Shelter: Mapping the Effects of Climate Change on Human Migration and Displacement*. United Nations University Institute for Environment and Human Security. May 2009. http://ciesin.columbia.edu/documents/clim-migr -report-june09_media.pdf.

Further Information

Books

Challen, Paul. *Migration in the 21st Century: How Will Globalization and Climate Change Affect Migration and Settlement?* St. Catharines, ON: Crabtree, 2010. This book covers the history of human migration and explores how climate change and economic globalization are causing more people than ever to relocate.

Fleischman, Paul. *Eyes Wide Open: Going behind the Environmental Headlines*. Somerville, MA: Candlewick, 2014. This book is a guide to understanding climate change as well as the roles politics and history play in current responses to the global climate crisis.

Kallen, Stuart A. *Running Dry: The Global Water Crisis*. Minneapolis: Twenty-First Century Books, 2015. One in nine people in the world does not have access to safe drinking water, and freshwater sources are dwindling due to climate change and other factors. Investigate the water crisis's causes, consequences, and potential solutions.

Lynas, Mark. *Six Degrees: Our Future on a Hotter Planet*. Washington, DC: National Geographic, 2008. Each chapter of this book considers the impacts of a rise in global temperature, from 1°F to 6°F (0.6°C to 3.3°C). From population shifts to national security crises, Lynas looks at climate change's long-term consequences for humanity.

McPherson, Stephanie Sammartino. *Arctic Thaw: Climate Change and the Global Race for Energy Resources*. Minneapolis: Twenty-First Century Books, 2014. As climate change transforms the top of the world, it is not only changing where people can live but exposing previously inaccessible resources. This book explores what a thawing Arctic means for the region's oil, natural gas, minerals, and wind and hydroelectric power.

Video

Nash, Michael P. *Climate Refugees*. LA Think Tank. Los Angeles: Preferred Content, 2010. This documentary film examines the lives of displaced people fleeing climate change around the world.

Websites

Climate Central: Surging Seas
  http://sealevel.climatecentral.org
  Click on coastal locations in the United States or search by zip code to see
  detailed maps of how different areas will be affected by sea level rise and
  flooding over time.

Earth: The Operator's Manual
  http://earththeoperatorsmanual.com
  This documentary series hosted by climate scientist Richard Alley aired on PBS
  and is now available online. It explores climate change and sustainable energy
  solutions.

National Snow and Ice Data Center
  http://nsidc.org
  This site provides updates on the state of Arctic ice, information on climate
  change, photographs, and daily images of Arctic sea ice.

United Nations Office for the Coordination of Humanitarian Affairs: Sahel Call for
  Humanitarian Aid
  http://www.unocha.org/sahel2015
  This interactive guide shows the extent of the humanitarian crisis in the Sahel
  and how climate change contributes to the situation.

US Global Change Research Program
  http://www.globalchange.gov/climate-change
  Learn more about the science of climate change and explore the impacts of
  climate change across the United States and the world.

Index

Photo Acknowledgments

The images in this book are used with the permission of: Phil Daquila/UNC News21/Newscom, pp. 5, 17; © Laura Westllund/Independent Picture Service, pp. 7, 22, 29, 37, 40 (bottom), 41, 65, 72; © Don Bartlett/Los Angeles Times/Getty Images, p. 14; AP Kent Porter/The Press Democrat/Photographer, p. 18; © Jonas Gratzer/LightRocket/Getty Images, pp. 21, 31; © Christian Aslund/Greenpeace Media, p. 27; AP Photo/Mohammed Seeneen, p. 33; © Boureima HAMA/AFP/Getty Images, p. 35; Conrad Duroseau/Zumapress.com/Newscom, p. 38; © Patrick T. Fallon/The Washington Post/Getty Images, p. 40 (top); © Seyllou Diallo/AFP/Getty Images, pp. 45, 64; © Debra L. Rothenberg/Getty Images, p. 47; © Menahem Kahana/AFP/Getty Images, p. 48; © Mohammed Asad/Pacific Press/LightRocket/Getty Images, p. 53; © Joe Raedle/Getty Images, p. 54; © Anders Birch/Redux, p. 58; AP Photo/Gerald Herbert, p. 59; REUTERS/Thomas Mukoya, p. 61; REUTERS, p. 69; © Jonathan Raa/NurPhoto/Corbis, p. 70; © Ratib Al Safadi/Andolu Agency/Getty Images, p. 74.

Front cover: © O. Alamany & E. Vicens/Corbis.

Back cover: © Gioppi/Dreamstime.com.

About the Author

Rebecca E. Hirsch has written about science and discovery in dozens of books for children and young adults. A former scientist, she holds a PhD in cellular and molecular biology from the University of Wisconsin. Hirsch lives in State College, Pennsylvania, with her husband, Rick, and their three daughters. You can learn more at her website: www.rebeccahirsch.com.